Dalkey Days

BOOKS BY STEVEN MOORE

A Reader's Guide to William Gaddis's "The Recognitions" (1982)
William Gaddis (1989; expanded edition 2015)
Ronald Firbank: An Annotated Bibliography of Secondary Materials
   (1996)
The Novel, An Alternative History: Beginnings to 1600 (2010)
The Novel, An Alternative History: 1600–1800 (2013)
My Back Pages: Reviews and Essays (2017)
Alexander Theroux: A Fan's Notes (2020)

BOOKS EDITED WITH AN INTRODUCTION
BY STEVEN MOORE

In Recognition of William Gaddis (with John Kuehl, 1984)
The Vampire in Verse: An Anthology (1985)
Edward Dahlberg, *Samuel Beckett's Wake and Other Uncollected Prose*
   (1989)
Ronald Firbank, *Complete Short Stories* (1990)
Ronald Firbank, *Complete Plays* (1994)
The Complete Fiction of W. M. Spackman (1997)
*Beerspit Night and Cursing: The Correspondence of Charles Bukowski
   and Sheri Martinelli* (2001)
Chandler Brossard, *Over the Rainbow? Hardly* (2005)
The Letters of William Gaddis (2013; expanded edition 2023)
On the Decay of Criticism: The Complete Essays of W. M. Spackman
   (2017)

Dalkey Days

A Memoir

STEVEN MOORE

ZEROGRAM PRESS

Los Angeles, 2023

ZEROGRAM PRESS
1147 El Medio Ave.
Pacific Palisades, CA 90272
Email: info@zerogrampress.com
Website: www.zerogrampress.com

Distributed by Small Press United / Independent Publishers Group
(800) 888-4741 / www.ipgbook.com

First Zerogram Press Edition 2023

Copyright ©2023 by Steven Moore

Book layout by Creative Publishing Book Design
Cover photo by Jeanne Fairbanks Gore, at Stuart Brent Books, Chicago,
    Summer 1991

Publisher's Cataloging-In-Publication Data:
Names: Moore, Steven, 1951- author.
Title: Dalkey days : a memoir / Steven Moore.
Description: Los Angeles, CA : Zerogram Press, 2023.
Identifiers: ISBN 978-1-953409-12-6 (paperback)
Subjects: LCSH: Book editors--Biography. | Editors--Biography. | Dalkey
    Archive Press. | Autobiography. | Illinois--Biography. | BISAC: BIOG-
    RAPHY & AUTOBIOGRAPHY / Editors, Journalists, Publishers.
    BIOGRAPHY & AUTOBIOGRAPHY / Personal Memoirs.
Classification: LCC PN149.9.M66 A3 2023 (print) | LCC PN149.9.M66
    (ebook) | DDC 070.41/092--dc23.

Printed in the United States of America

Contents

PART 1
My Dalkey Days

Back cover of *A Dalkey Archive Reader*, no. 1 (Spring/Summer 1993)

1

I FIRST LEARNED of John O'Brien in 1981. Having heard that I would be publishing a book on William Gaddis the following year, Professor John Kuehl of New York University wrote to invite me to contribute an essay to a collection of essays on Gaddis that he was assembling, which I did. In fact, I gave him so many suggestions about its possible contents that he asked me to co-edit the volume, which was published in 1984 as *In Recognition of William Gaddis*. He told me that, coincidentally, a new journal called the *Review of Contemporary Fiction* was planning a half-issue on Gaddis for the summer of 1982. We conducted an interview by mail with Gaddis in January 1982, intended for our book, but Kuehl was disappointed at its brevity and offered it to O'Brien, who added it to the Summer 1982 issue, along with a Gaddis bibliography that I had compiled at O'Brien's request. (I think it came by way of Kuehl, not direct.)

Aside from its large format, copied from *Vort* magazine (1972–76)— and O'Brien would always *copy* formats that he liked, rather than adapt them—one odd thing about the *Review* struck me, and in retrospect was a red flag. On a page upfront providing submission requirements, O'Brien insisted that contributors must send "perfect copy"—meaning their manuscripts had to be immaculate: no typos, no errors, no handwritten corrections: *perfect* copy. I had never seen that requirement before. Few writers are expert typists—this was back when virtually all were still using typewriters—so this struck me as ridiculously unrealistic, a quality O'Brien would often display in later years.

In 1984, having taken a great interest in a novelist-friend of Gaddis's named Chandler Brossard, I wrote to O'Brien to ask if I could guest-edit an issue on him. He said he was familiar with Brossard (though vaguely enough that I suspect Brossard was only a name to him), and gave me the go-ahead. I assembled the contents over the next year and a half, and the issue was published in the spring of 1987, by which time *RCF* had been redesigned to its now-familiar 6 x 9 format. (I was studying for my PhD

at the time, first at Denver University, then at Rutgers in New Jersey.)
On the basis of that, O'Brien then asked me to co-edit an issue called
"Novelist as Critic," which amounted to inviting our favorite writers to
submit a literary essay, for $200. William Gaddis turned me down, but
a fresh-faced writer named David Foster Wallace accepted. This was
published in fall 1988, along with a half-dozen book reviews of mine,
which I had been contributing to the *Review* since 1986.[1] Based on all
this—which in retrospect was a kind of sequential audition—he asked me
to join Dalkey Archive Press/*Review of Contemporary Fiction*.

2

John O'Brien (1945–2020) began the press in 1984, he later told me, as
a result of the success of the *Review* (as we called it in-house). Because
it was a 501(c)3 nonprofit organization, it was funded by both the
National Endowment for the Arts and the Illinois Arts Council, and had
amassed enough subscribers—especially libraries, which he worked very
hard on—that by 1984 he found himself with a financial surplus. So he
decided to start a paperback reprint line, named after Flann O'Brien's
last novel, *The Dalkey Archive* (1964). That was his first mistake. I had
read the novel years before because my idol James Joyce is a character in
it, but few people recognized the allusion, or knew what it meant, plus
it was hard to remember and often mispronounced—Donkey Archive
Press being my favorite. A devoted—nay, worshipful—admirer of Gilbert
Sorrentino, his first reprint was *Splendide-Hôtel*, in a split edition: $3.95
paperback, and a jacketless hardback edition intended for libraries priced
at a whopping $20: the equivalent today of $50. He stole the cover design
from Gallimard's paperback line, which he always admired. I remember
a few years later, while manning the Dalkey booth at the annual ABA
(booksellers' convention), two name-tagged representatives from Gallimard
spotted our early titles and looked at one another with widened eyes. *Quel
outrage!* That was his second mistake, for American booksellers didn't like
the design, or the cover stock used (which soiled easily), or the absence
of any description on the back cover. As he published more reprints over
the next few years, he numbered them under the misassumption (third

---

1 These, and virtually all other reviews and essays mentioned hereafter, can be
found in *My Back Pages* (Los Angeles: Zerogram Press, 2017).

mistake) that some people will want to collect the set. They were personal favorites, but little known to anyone else: *Cadenza* by Ralph Cusack—whose heirs O'Brien couldn't locate, so he published it anyway and hoped for the best (no one ever came forward), *Wall to Wall* by Douglas Woolf, *Season at Coole* by Michael Stephens, *Out of Focus* by Alf Mac Lochlainn (my favorite of these early reprints), *Some Instructions to My Wife . . .* by Stanley Crawford, and two novels by Nicholas Mosley (who shared the other half of that Gaddis *RCF* issue). The texts were offset from the originals, and most came with an afterword O'Brien solicited from some good names: Sorrentino (on Cusack), Robert Creeley (on Sorrentino), Thomas McGonigle (on Stephens), and Steven Weisenburger (on Mosley's *Accident*). These books didn't sell well, but that wasn't a great concern at the time: production costs were low, and they were largely covered by the NEA and IAC surplus, though I don't think O'Brien told them he was using their money for books. He was content just to get these favorites back into print, and publicly vowed to keep them there.

The afterwords and the *Review* were typeset by the only other employee of Dalkey at the time, a wonderful older woman named Shirley Geever (1942–2015), a self-assured cat-lover. She had been the department secretary at the school O'Brien taught at during this period, Illinois Benedictine College in Lisle, Illinois, and he worked out a deal with the school to use her part-time for *RCF* at first, and then for Dalkey. She had no interest in the kind of fiction he published, but she was a superb typist and an efficient office manager until, like me, she became disgusted with O'Brien and quit in 1996, the same time I did. The official place of publication was 1817 79th Avenue, Elmwood Park—an upscale suburb of Chicago. John had converted his basement into an office, most of which was taken up by shelves and shelves of books, thousands of them. It was a dark room—he hated overhead lighting, even disabled it at his school office—and at his messy desk he did all the copyediting and proofreading. One of his kids would sometimes answer when someone called the press. The earliest paperbacks were shipped to his house and stored in another part of the basement, then taken out, a few boxes at a time, to Illinois Benedictine, where orders were filled. Most of them came not from bookstores but from individuals.

In 1986 he decided to start publishing original books, hardbacks with dust-jackets intended for bookstores. The first was a collection of essays and reviews by Paul Metcalf entitled *Where Do You Put the Horse?* Metcalf had been the subject of one of the earliest issues of the *Review*, and in addition to a small trade printing—priced at $20 when comparable books cost $15—O'Brien offered a limited edition of 26 signed and numbered copies, only about half of which had sold by the time I left. (We did only one more limited edition, for Alexander Theroux's *Lollipop Trollops* in 1992, which sold out quickly because it was co-signed by cover artist Edward Gorey.) The following year he ventured a few more titles by American writers— Thomas McGonigle's *Corpse Dream of N. Petkov* (March 1987), Kenneth Tindall's *Banks of the Sea* (October), Gilbert Sorrentino's *Rose Theatre* (November)—and two more reprints: *Too Much Flesh and Jabez* (April) by Coleman Dowell, whom he knew well, and Dalkey's first book by a woman, Luisa Valenzuela's *He Who Searches* (May). But the most significant new book O'Brien published in 1987 was an unassuming French novel that played a huge role in Dalkey's subsequent direction: *Our Share of Time* by Yves Navarre, as translated by a young Philadelphian named Dominic Di Bernardi.

When submitting the manuscript, Di Bernardi mentioned that funding was available from the French Ministry of Culture, which would pay for the author's advance, the translator's fee, and provide some money toward production costs and marketing. Like the funding for the *Review*, this meant publication was almost risk-free: Dalkey's production costs were low enough that selling only a small number of copies would be enough to break even and start generating profits. Like the man who discovered the goose that laid golden eggs, O'Brien welcomed further French translations from Di Bernardi and others, which accounts for the large number of French titles on Dalkey's list from 1987 onward. Shortly after I moved out to Lisle in 1988—I arrived on a dark, stormy Halloween, foreboding in retrospect—O'Brien showed me a tentative publishing schedule for the next two years. In addition to actual titles, each season had an untitled "French novel" penciled in. I said something like "Wow, you must really like French fiction"; he chuckled and admitted he did them mostly because the French Ministry would pay for them. He did indeed like French fiction, but it was mostly New Wave writers: Robbe-Grillet, Pinget, Butor, Simon, Duras, and others featured in a book he commissioned, Leon S. Roudiez's *French Fiction Revisited* (1991, a revision of his 1972 book *French Fiction Today*). But it was mostly the financial cushion provided by funding that induced him to publish in quick succession Pierre Albert-Birot's *Grabinoulor* (March 1987), Claude Ollier's *Mis-en-Scène* (May 1988), Maurice Roche's *Compact* (October 1988), Muriel Cerf's *Street Girl* (November 1988), Marc Cholodenko's *Mordechai Schamz* (December 1988), and several novels by Raymond Queneau: *Pierre Mon Ami* (March 1988), *Odile* (December 1988), and *The Last Days* (October 1990). Soon he welcomed translations from other languages, as long as they were underwritten by foreign ministries, and in the years following my departure Dalkey became primarily a publisher of translations as O'Brien traveled the world soliciting funding.

He became celebrated as a champion of literature in translation; while I wouldn't say that was just a front, virtually every writer he praised in my presence wrote in English. Nor did he settle for partial financial support, as in the past; he later expected ministries and donors to cover all production costs, which he wildly exaggerated, to ensure a profit before a single copy was sold. Some would call that a smart business strategy, but others would wonder if that is appropriate for a tax-exempt nonprofit cultural organization.

3

Such was Dalkey when I joined, though my joining was a gradual process. I began merely as an advisor to the press. In 1987, when I was still at Rutgers finishing my PhD, I suggested O'Brien consider for publication a novel David Markson had shared with me entitled *Wittgenstein's Mistress*, which he had been trying to place with a publisher for years, racking up fifty-four rejections.[2] O'Brien liked it as much as I did, published it in May 1988, and it became Dalkey's first "best-seller," albeit by small press standards. The first printing (700-800 copies) sold quickly, and was followed by a second in July. We brought out a paperback in February 1990, which has been continuously reprinted since then. British rights were sold, then translation rights to several countries. O'Brien proposed that I become a kind of East Coast liaison for the press, and offered to pay me $100 a month for helping out with proofreading and other tasks—which as a poor graduate student I was happy to accept. Eager to get his money's worth, he also asked me to supply reader reports on novels he was considering, such as Evelyn E. Sullivan's *The Dead Magician* (published in October 1989) and Thomas McGonigle's *Going to Patchogue* (not published until January 1992), though I pleaded I was too busy completing my degree—studying for a Spanish proficiency exam, finishing my dissertation—for that much work. He also mailed me numerous long letters during this time, going on at stupefying length about his vision for the company and the nature of the commitment I needed to make.

---

2 The list is reproduced on p. 163 of *Lists of Note: An Eclectic Collection Deserving of a Wider Audience*, ed. Shaun Usher (San Francisco: Chronicle Books, 2015). I had made Markson's acquaintance a few years earlier because of his connection with William Gaddis.

One task raised another red flag. In spring 1988 he sent me a list of a hundred or so independent bookstores and wanted me to call and ask for the store's buyer, and then ask them if it would be permissible to send them Dalkey's fall 1988 catalog. I told O'Brien that I didn't think that was necessary: I had worked at a Denver bookstore in my mid-twenties, and even opened and ran my own bookstore from 1978 to 1981, and assured him that booksellers always welcomed publishers' catalogs. But he insisted a personal touch was necessary: after receiving a personal call from us, a bookstore owner would be more likely to pay special attention to the catalog when it arrived and, he hoped, place a large order. With list in hand, I dutifully began calling them, with predictable results. Most simply said "Sure," but sometimes the book-buyer was out or unavailable, necessitating a follow-up call. When I actually reached the owner, they usually just said, "Yeah, send it to us and we'll take a look" and hung up. Other times, I had to wait while whoever answered searched for the manager, who finally came to the phone with the unmistakable tone of someone interrupted from work, and their curt response had a "Why are you calling me about this?" tone that confirmed my suspicions. I made it through about three-fourths of the list—my phone bill was enormous, eating up that $100 monthly stipend—and then mailed it back to O'Brien with checks against the names of stores that agreed to a catalog. He grumbled later that a few names toward the end of the list were no longer operative; I can't remember what excuse I gave for that, but it was the first of many ill-conceived, time&money-wasting tasks that I had to perform in later years. (Examples will follow.)

I never planned to go into publishing. A few months before receiving my PhD in May 1988, I began applying to colleges that were advertising for positions in modern and/or American literature. I didn't start at the top with places like Harvard or Yale, but rather with middle-tiered colleges like (I think) Rice University, Franklin & Marshall, places like that, but with no luck: despite the fact that I had already published two books with university presses, had a contract for a third (my dissertation), and had published several essays in peer-reviewed journals, I couldn't even get an interview, much less a job offer. I've often wondered why. At the time, many universities were allowing the positions vacated by retiring professors to go unfilled, relying instead on considerably cheaper adjunct professors, so maybe that was it. And/or the multiculturalism tide was rising, and as a straight white man who wrote about WASP-ish authors I wasn't exactly welcome at the barbecue. Or it could have been for something as simple as commencing my college education at a community college. Not wanting to spend months applying to increasingly smaller schools, or to join the ranks of nomadic adjuncts, I looked around for alternatives. I interviewed for a job at the MLA Bibliography office, but I did so poorly that they didn't call back, nor do I blame them: I would describe my interview as catatonic.

A soul-crushing romantic disappointment in 1985—the last straw in a series ever since Susan Duralia turned me down for a 9th-grade dance—plunged me into a deep depression that lasted for the next ten years, and affects me to this day. So when O'Brien offered me a full-time job in the summer of 1988, I took it. He had recently sold the *Review*'s archives to the Stanford University library, which allowed him to offer me $12,000 a year—roughly equivalent to $30K today. Given the lack of response to my university job-hunting, and my disastrous performance at the MLA office, and with no other options in mind, I figured a quiet job at a small press in the Midwest would be better than becoming a mailman (which I actually considered). I was no fun to be around, but I was confident I could do the job: like a functioning alcoholic, I was a functioning depressive, and in fact keeping busy with one writing project after another was the best way to keep my depression at bay. That and listening to music, which has always been my alcohol, my drug.

During my years at Dalkey I was a workaholic: I put in long hours, took work home at night, worked weekends, rarely called in sick, and never took a vacation. Though I am proud of the books I published there, it was the wrong place for a depressive to work: aside from Dalkey's continuous financial problems and increasingly toxic atmosphere, it was an uphill battle getting our books noticed by reviewers, handled by distributors, placed in bookstores, and so forth. I hated having to man a booth in suit and title and forced smile at the annual trade shows (the ABA for booksellers, the ALA for librarians, the MLA for English professors), hated sales conferences where I had to hawk our forthcoming books to distributors—though I was told I was very good at it—hated the visits to bored book-review editors, giving them every reason I could conjure up to review our books, usually with no results. But mostly I grew to hate working with O'Brien.

I had met him only once before I went to work for him. In 1987 or so, I met *RCF* contributor Irving Malin in New York for something and he introduced me to O'Brien, there for something or other. (I've never kept a journal, so I'm relying on my fading memory for most of this.) He seemed OK, rather low-keyed, a few years older than I (42 to my 36), and with his ever-present briefcase (which he took everywhere he went, and I mean *everywhere*, as though it were an appendage). But after I moved out to Illinois and started working with him, I realized we had little in common, aside from some shared literary interests, and that I didn't particularly like him; he's not the kind of person I normally would have become friends with (though I was in no mood then for socializing). Though only six years older, he seemed to belong to the previous generation. He was married with four kids, lived in the suburbs, dressed conservatively, smoked, wore his hair short, drove aggressively, and disliked rock music. His friends called him Jack, but he remained John to me.

One of the first things that turned me off was his habit of lying; he's one of those people who feel lying is a normal part of social intercourse, whereas I consider it one of the worst things you can do, especially to someone you know. Here's a defining example that I've never forgotten: in spring 1989 we published a special issue of the *Review* called "New French Fiction," mostly filled with chapter-length translations by Di Bernardi. (After copyediting the issue, I told O'Brien my favorite pieces were selections from recent novels by Jacques Roubaud and Patrick Grainville, and he promptly engaged Dom to acquire rights and translate them for us.) Near the back of the issue there was a 23-page feature called "Book Reviewing in America: A Forum." O'Brien had asked a large number of book-review editors to respond to a "deliberately provocative diatribe on the state of American publishing and reviewing" by a visiting French professor named Patrice Roussel—a pseudonym O'Brien sometimes used, especially for book reviews. (Using a fake name is a kind of lying, isn't it?) Sitting in his gloomy basement one afternoon, he told me that some of the editors called him and asked who exactly this French professor was, and he *laughed* as he told me of the lies he spun to these honest, trusting people. Even the "forum" was a kind of lie: he didn't really care what these editors thought; he just wanted to bring Dalkey Archive to their attention, to flatter them by publishing them in his journal in the hope they would respond more positively when Dalkey books arrived on their desk for review. O'Brien had this Chicago gangster "I do you a favor, you do me one" mentality, convinced the personal touch was how you got things done—like that bookseller-calling task described earlier. This doesn't work: I could give examples of book-review editors who ignored the books we hyped during a visit, only to review another of our books a year later when we deliberately *didn't* visit them; or ignored the titles we talked up, only to review one of the titles we mentioned only in passing.

I was also turned off that afternoon by O'Brien's titanic arrogance. This little-known professor at a little-known Catholic college working out of his basement in a little-known Chicago suburb thought he knew better than all these experienced professionals, smart people who had been actually working in the book-review business for years. I've just reread the forum and am surprised how thoughtful and well-informed their responses are. Nor did they dislodge his fixed notion of how reviewing worked; Mitchell Levitas, then editor of the *New York Times Book Review*, wrote, "As for

'Patrice Roussel' her comments belong more properly in the *National Lampoon*," but Patrice stuck to her opinion.

The first time O'Brien got visibly mad at me was when I *didn't* lie to someone. A reporter from Long Island's *Newsday* called me to say he was writing a feature on Thomas McGonigle's autobiographical *Going to Patchogue*, and asked what the print run was, and I told him (1300 copies, I think). Consequently, he reported that readers may have trouble finding the book in stores because we were *only* printing 1300 copies, which was a reasonable number for small and university presses. "Why did you tell him that?!" O'Brien stormed when he saw the piece. "You should have told him we hadn't decided yet!" But we had. Call me unworldly, but my first instinct isn't to lie. (I soon learned that most publishers evade or exaggerate their print-runs.)

At the aforementioned trade shows, I would stand there dumbfounded as O'Brien lied to fellow publishers: he told the editor of Fromm International that he sent one of their books to three different reviewers trying to get a positive review, but had to settle for the final, ho-hum one—whereas in truth he had sent the novel only to that one reviewer, his old friend Jack Byrne. (The book in question was Sorrentino's *Red the Fiend*, his only bad novel IMO). He apologized to the editor of *The Columbia History of the American Novel* for a negative review in our Summer 1992 issue by blaming the reviewer, whereas in fact *he* had written the review under his Roussel nom de plume. I said nothing, for I assumed he at least didn't lie to me, but when I eventually caught him in a bare-faced lie, that pretty much ended my respect for him.

This incident provides another illuminating example of his ways and means:

At the 1993 ABA convention, I picked up a marketing item from a British publisher called Harvill, promoting their forthcoming books with little features about them, and shared it with O'Brien. He decided we should steal their design and do something just like it—and I mean literally steal: the oversized item was 30 x 42 centimeters, apparently a standard size in England but not among U.S. printers, but O'Brien didn't care: he wanted it *exactly* the same size, even though that would cost extra. Ours measured 11 5/8 by 16 3/8 inches, and an example is reproduced on the next page not only because it's now quite rare, but also because I wrote the unsigned lead article on the left, which was the seed that would grow a decade later into my two-trunked tree *The Novel: An Alternative History*, the first volume of which—another trivial coincidence—used as its cover art the same image I used for the "New French Fiction" issue mentioned above, from a print I had bought while working at ABC Books circa 1976.

Inside: Robert Coover   Carole Maso   Gilbert Sorrentino

Dalkey News

Volume Two Number One   Fall 1993

Dalkey Archive: The Tradition of the New

OVER THE YEARS, Dalkey Archive has acquired a reputation for doing untraditional, non-mainstream novels. This is considered a virtue by some, a defect by others. What is often ignored in such discussions, however, is what "traditional" in fiction actually means. The novel as most people know it—that is, a realistic narrative driven by a strong plot and peopled with well-rounded characters—is actually a fairly recent development in the novel's 2000-year history. Instead of enjoying a brief fad and then losing favor, as did the epistolary novel, the realistic novel invented by the French novelist Balzac in the 1830s became the favored form for many writers and readers, and since then has come to be thought of as the "norm" in fiction. Instead, it is a late, rather simplistic deviation from the development of prose fiction, and one concerned less with technique and form than with pleasing audiences and enriching authors and publishers.

The novel began as something considerably different. The earliest novels were Greek romances and Roman satires, where the plot was a mere convenience that allowed the author to engage in rhetorical display, literary criticism, socio-political commentary, digressions, and so on. It was an elastic form that made room for interpolated poems, stories within stories, and parodies, where the realistic and the fantastic blend together. (In other words, "magic realism" was not invented twenty years ago by the Latin-American "Boom" writers, but instead has *always* been a property of the novel.) This kind of novel, as exemplified by Petronius (*The Satyricon*) and Lucius Apuleius (*The Golden Ass*), was the norm for 18 centuries, and has its counterpart in the fiction of the Middle East (*The Thousand and One Arabian Nights*), Japan (Lady Murasaki's *Tale of Genji*), and China (*The Dream of the Red Chamber*). None of these resembles the kind of novel on the *New York Times* best-seller list.

When the European novel was revived in the Renaissance, it showed its classical heritage. The novels of such 16th-century writers as Rabelais and Cervantes have the same kind of "magic realism" as found in Petronius or Scheherazade's tales and continue their tradition of rhetorical display and formal inventiveness. (At one point in *Don Quixote*, the knight and his squire actually come across a copy of *Don Quixote* in a bookshop: the kind of blurring between reality and fiction more often associated with today's metafictionists has, again, always been a property of the novel.) In *Tristram Shandy* (1759-67), Laurence Sterne expanded the novel's possibilities to encompass virtually anything the writer wanted to do. These novelists, like most that followed, were learned scholars: they knew the prose tradition that preceded them and, by way of homage and parody, kept the tradition alive. Even when plot was allowed a greater role in fiction, as in Fielding's *Tom Jones*, the classical heritage was kept in mind: Fielding called his novel "a comic epic in prose"—thereby evoking epic poets like Homer and Virgil—and gave his novel a three-part structure rooted in classical architecture. Novelists like Fielding and Thackeray (*Vanity Fair*) continued to confide in the reader in asides (a mainstay of classic drama) and to allude to classic models. When Joyce modeled his *Ulysses* on Homer's *Odyssey*, he was following a time-honored tradition, even though his ill-educated critics accused him of "killing" the novel.

Throughout its 2000-year history, the novel has valued innovation (one of the meanings of the word *novel* is "new"), taking advantage of the form's elasticity to try new approaches, new techniques. The novel has always been a workshop, not a mausoleum. Yet for some reason, the straightforward realistic novel invented by Balzac and popularized by numerous lesser talents ever since achieved ascendance in the 19th century and began squeezing out more inventive fictions. Hawthorne complained of the popular novelists who were, even in his day, claiming most book sales and review coverage, and Melville had to give up writing inventive novels like *Moby-Dick* and *The Confidence Man* due to critical misunderstanding and the reading public's desire for simpler fare. At that point, fiction writing branched into two streams—the commercial one of realistic fiction for mass audiences and literary fiction for more discerning readers—and, ironically, the stream that deviated from the long tradition of innovative fiction became the "main" stream, while the older tradition became a misunderstood tributary.

Dalkey Archive is intent on fostering modern practitioners of that older tradition. Some of our authors, like Felipe Alfau, Djuna Barnes, Chandler Brossard, and Rikki Ducornet, continue the exuberant episodic fiction of Cervantes and Sterne. Others keep the novel tradition fresh by devising new formal challenges for it: the Paris-based OuLiPo group (Le Ouvroir de Littérature Potentielle—The Workshop for Potential Literature) is devoted to precisely this task, and includes such authors of ours as Raymond Queneau (its co-founder), Jacques Roubaud, and Harry Mathews; other of our authors follow Oulipian practices, especially Gilbert Sorrentino and Paul West (in *Gala*). Many of our women authors are exploring new kinds of female fiction (especially Marguerite Young, Julieta Campos, and Carole Maso), breaking away from traditional forms of narration. Every author on our list is pushing the envelope of fiction in one way or another, intent on renewing the genre and providing state-of-the-art fiction for connoisseurs of literature.

Don Quixote in his library

SISTER CARRIE

edited by

LAUREN FAIRBANKS

THOROUGHLY MODERN CARRIE

LAUREN FAIRBANKS's *Sister Carrie*, just published by Dalkey ($19.95. ISBN 1-56478-035-X), is on one level an update of Theodore Dreiser's 1900 novel. How would a Carrie Meeber of the 1990s differ from her 1890s original? Not by much, the author feels: "The similarity between the two Carries is the ability to move from one world to another without a backward glance," she told us recently. "I see this door-closing as a modern trait. This is why Dreiser's Carrie is so modern. Guilt doesn't seem to be in her vocabulary. Both protagonists are success stories because of this ability. It's very pragmatic: as they move forward in life, they throw away any baggage and adopt new 'truths' as circumstances change. (It's very convenient and sensible; the downside is a human piece is missing.) They both prostitute themselves. Dreiser's Carrie seems better at getting out of the muck.

"Chicago and acting are also common denominators," Fairbanks continues. "The thing I love about the title of Dreiser's book is that she is hardly ever referred to as 'Sister Carrie,' but being a sister is what gets her going to Chicago in the first place."

Fairbanks's Carrie leaves her stifling Florida home for Chicago, where she enters the related fields of advertising and prostitution. Her mysterious disappearance is the focus of much of the novel; as an unflappable narrator makes inquiries into her bizarre life, a cartoonish, hyperkinetic, blaring street world envelops the reader.

The novel has already received

(See CARRIE, page 3)

In addition to the nonstandard size, O'Brien insisted we use the exact same paper, a heavy gray textured stock: quite beautiful but also quite expensive. Each issue highlighted three or four recent books of ours, along with a short essay or two: this one featured Rikki Ducornet's "Robert Coover's Cosmical Ogress" and one by O'Brien on Sorrentino's *Aberration of Starlight* called "The Most Teachable Book in Literature." It was intended for English professors—we had purchased a few mailing lists along the way—who, we hoped, would either adopt the books for classroom use or recommend them to their libraries. (There was a handy "Library Order Form" on page 3.) Apart from these two contributors, I wrote all the other pieces, and worked with Shirley Geever to design the thing, both of which were time-consuming tasks. It would have been worth it if it actually resulted in a bump in sales for these titles, but that didn't seem to be the case. At least we didn't lose money on it: though expensive to design, print, and mail, the item was underwritten (according to a box at the bottom of page 2) by a grant from the Lila Wallace-Reader's Digest Literary Publishers Development Program, more of which anon.

After three or four issues over a year or two, I suspected the *Dalkey News* wasn't working, and went into O'Brien's office and suggested we discontinue it. He fired back that it was indeed working, and had generated $10,000 in recent sales. I instinctively apologized—he was much more abreast of sales than I was—but noticed he wasn't gloating, and even seemed a bit embarrassed by my apology. As I walked back to my office I started thinking about that enormous sales figure, which didn't sound right. I gathered the three or four issues we had done so far, jotted down the featured titles, then got out the printouts of monthly sales for the last year and a half, and soon realized that while a few of the titles had sold a few more copies than usual—and I literally mean a few: four or five copies in some months rather than the usual two or three—I realized the aggregate of those slight increases, which could be attributed to almost anything, couldn't possibly add up to $10,000: a suspiciously round figure that O'Brien obviously pulled out of the air (if not from lower). As proud as Lucifer, as confident as Trump, he never admitted he made a mistake or confessed that one of his many untethered marketing schemes had failed. (Which they all did.) A less depressed person would have gone back to his office and called him a liar while waving those sales sheets in the air. But I didn't. I'm not the confrontational type, I already knew he was a liar, had already been losing respect for him, so I shook my head and got back to work. A few months later, O'Brien mentioned in passing that we should shutter the *Dalkey News*.

4

I'll hit pause on this airing of grievances to focus on the things I liked most about working at Dalkey: the reprinting of worthy out-of-print novels, the publication of new authors, and the near-total control of the *Review of Contemporary Fiction*, which allowed me to celebrate many of my favorite authors, to review as many books I wanted in our back pages, and to assign books I felt should be reviewed. Looking back, I'm surprised to see that at least two-thirds of the books Dalkey published between 1988 and 1996 were my choices or suggestions, and maybe half of featured authors in the *Review*. To avoid interrupting the narrative/chronological flow, I've listed my acquisitions in part 2.

One book I suggested to O'Brien while still at Rutgers proved to be a turning point in Dalkey's fortunes, and may have even saved it: Felipe Alfau's *Locos: A Comedy of Gestures*, originally published in 1936 (see part 3 for the full story). I began reading it in the spring of 1988, was blown away by its opening pages, and after reading more mailed it to O'Brien, telling him he has to read it. He too was impressed, and since he had only four French novels lined up for the fall list, he decided to add it. Appearing at the end of 1988, it attracted some attention and sold OK, partly due to the publication of Mary McCarthy's afterword in the *New York Review of Books*, but it was Alfau's next novel, the previously unpublished *Chromos*, that put Dalkey on the map. Published in the spring of 1990, that novel was even better received, and—much to our and the book industry's surprise—became a finalist for the National Book Award in fiction, the first time for small, nonprofit press book. Two of the judges wanted it to win—Paul West and William H. Gass—but it lost to Charles Johnson's *Middle Passage*. But Alfau's novels proved to be a goldmine: paperback rights to both were sold to Vintage, British rights to Viking/Penguin, and translation rights to a variety of foreign publishers. Each came with a large check, which—since Alfau had waived royalties—was all ours. (I never learned the amounts, but we must have received 20 or 30 thousand dollars between 1990 and 1993.)

More importantly in the long run, we attracted the attention of several nonprofit literary organizations. Having secured funding from the NEA and IAC early on, O'Brien was eager—make that obsessed—to find more foundations to help, but our previous efforts had failed. One of the first bootless tasks O'Brien assigned me after my arrival in Illinois was to research funding possibilities. I spent two days at a small office in downtown Chicago devoted to foundations, plowing through reference books and annual reports from hundreds of organizations. As far as I could tell, no foundations offered support to small presses: there were plenty that bestowed grants on individual writers—the Guggenheim Foundation, the Rockefeller Foundation, the newish MacArthur Foundation—and some helped with literacy programs and such, but no one seemed interested in underwriting publishers. The only possibility I came across was the Lannan Foundation, but they didn't respond to my beseeching letter. After reporting back to O'Brien, he decided to focus on Illinois foundations and charitable organizations, and sent me back to that foundation library to compile a list of a hundred or so places whose activities and mission statements included anything remotely to do with books or reading or culture. I came up with a list, we sent letters out, but the only responses we received were letters chiding us for not paying closer attention to their mission statements.

But after *Chromos* was short-listed for the NBA, I learned that when it comes to foundations, you don't go to them, they come to you. We started receiving invitations to submit grant proposals from such organizations as the Andrew W. Mellon Foundation and the Lila Wallace-Reader's Digest Fund. The Lannan Foundation took notice of us after we published the Alexander Theroux/Paul West number of the *Review* (Spring 1991)—two faves of mine that O'Brien had no interest in—and not only awarded fellowship prizes to several of our authors in the early 1990s (Theroux, West, Sorrentino, Carole Maso, Rikki Ducornet) but underwrote various Dalkey endeavors later in the 1990s.

Back to 1988. Unbeknownst to me, Dalkey was heading toward a financial crisis. Aside from *Wittgenstein's Mistress*, none of the early books sold much, and before *Locos* was added, the line-up for Fall 1988 consisted of four French translations, all of which sold poorly. The Spring 1989 list was not promising sales-wise: the first two novels in Nicholas Mosley's Catastrophe Practice series, and a pet project of mine, Alan Ansen's *Contact Highs: Selected Poems*. By this point O'Brien had apparently used up the Stanford library money, and while he didn't confide in me, there were obvious signs something was wrong. I received a phone call from an irate Bernard Gotfryd, who provided the cover photo for an Edward Dahlberg book we published later in 1989, complaining that Dalkey's $100 check bounced. On another occasion, an impolite guy from a collection agency one of our printers had hired called me at home regarding unpaid printing bills. (All the preceding books were hardcovers, which are obviously more expensive to produce than paperbacks.)

It didn't occur to me until a few years later that, had I not become involved with Dalkey, it would not have published *Wittgenstein's Mistress*, *Locos*, or *Chromos*—that is, its first (and perennial) best-seller, and two novels that not only earned tens of thousands of dollars in sales and licensing, but attracted the untold thousands of dollars that foundations would soon start granting us. Without those three books, with a bank account in arrears, O'Brien would have probably halted his book publishing program in early 1989, or return to reprinting an occasional paperback favorite, as at the beginning. The first book of O'Brien's that sold well was Nicholas Mosley's *Hopeful Monsters*, published in late 1991, but without the three books I brought in, Dalkey might not have lasted until then. It sounds self-aggrandizing to spell it out, but it looks like I saved Dalkey Archive and guaranteed its future, doesn't it.

I even came up with the Dalkey logo. In 1989 or so, O'Brien decided we needed one, so Shirley showed us a page of dingbats, symbols, and devices available on her machine. I pointed to one that looked like a capital D with an A inside, but also evoking a Daedalian labyrinth, suitable for our sometimes labyrinthine novels.

5

Another thing I liked about working at Dalkey was designing covers, something neither I or O'Brien had any background or talent for. Money was too tight to hire outside designers, so when O'Brien began to publish hardbacks, he based his covers on those of New Directions from the 1950s and 1960s. They were typically full-bleed black and white photos, with little more than the author and title (no blurbs or hype), like these:

Consequently, the earliest Dalkey dust-jackets looked like these:

O'Brien wanted pay homage to New Directions and Grove Press, who did some similar portrait covers, though the gesture was probably lost on everyone but the literary cognoscenti. The other advantage was that black and white was considerably cheaper than color covers. Before I even joined full-time O'Brien welcomed my suggestions for cover art, especially for the books I had recommended. (David Markson provided the photo for his novel, but I found and arranged for the Dahlberg photo.) From about 1989 onward, I "designed" most of Dalkey's covers, aside from a few translations whose covers were carried over from the originals (Julián Ríos's *Larva*, Alain Vircondelet's Duras biography). Though not a particular admirer of the New Directions aesthetic, or a believer that covers made much difference to serious literary readers, I didn't mind it and followed the "house style" of full-bleed photos for the next few years, like these:

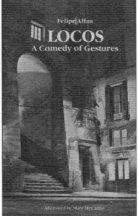
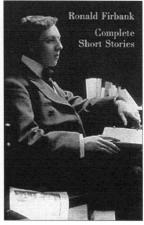

For new books, I always accommodated authors who had provided their own cover art, enthusiastically in some cases (Edward Gorey's cover for Alexander Theroux's *Lollipop Trollops*, Rikki Ducornet's covers, Eva Kuryluk's *Century 21*, Timothy d'Arch Smith's *Alembic*—another rare color cover), less so in other cases (those by Lauren Fairbanks, Carole Maso, Aurelie Sheehan, and June Akers Seese).

Gaining confidence, I got a little fancier with some covers, such as Chantal Chawaf's sexually violent *Redemption*, featuring a dictionary entry for "redemption"; Jack Green's *Fire the Bastards!*, which I pasted up from my Gaddis collection to complement the text's DIY aesthetic; and Christine Brooke-Rose's *Amalgamemnon*, created on my first word processor (an Amiga 1200, I think, with a 13" monitor), supplied by the university:

In 1990 I fell under the spell of Robert Longo's *Men in the Cities* series, and obtained rights to use two of them for two of O'Brien's books:[3]

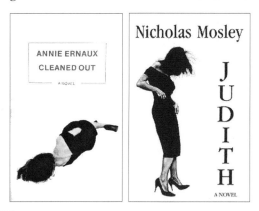

3 One day after adding the *Cleaned Out* image to my manuscript, Ernaux won the Nobel Prize for Literature. I vaguely recall copyediting it, and liking the short novel. A shame Dalkey let it go o.p. years ago.

I was especially proud of the cover I created for Robert Coover's dark, unsettling *A Night at the Movies*, which Coover loved, but which Dalkey replaced for its second printing after I left. You be the judge; as Hamlet tells his mother, "Look here upon this picture, and on this:"

O'Brien stuck with black and white covers until 1994—I remember telling him I had an appealing color image for James Merrill's *(Diblos) Notebook* and asking if it was time to make the jump to color, which he declined—but beginning in 1995 we not only started doing some color covers, but began hiring outsiders to design them, which was largely fine by me because they obviously were better qualified. (Not so fine with me was office-manager/boss's girlfriend Angela Weaser's loud, garish transformation of my quiet, elegant cover for Gertrude Stein's *Making of Americans* featuring the Dolly Sisters; Steven Meyer, who wrote the introduction, was so disgusted that he didn't speak to me for a month.) On the other hand, the change to color was a sad concession: when O'Brien began with the black and white covers, he not only wanted to evoke the best independent presses of the past, but to make our books stand out from the colorful mob on bookstore tables. He *wanted* them to look different. But by 1995, he wanted our books to blend in, to look like everyone else's. The first Coover image above was identifiably a Dalkey Archive book; the second could be from anybody.

6

In spring 1992 Illinois Benedictine College told O'Brien they no longer wanted to house the press—they accused him of operating a private business—and we moved into office space in Naperville, a few miles west of Lisle. Around that time O'Brien left his wife, so he moved his huge personal library into the second-floor office, and bought new furniture with the money Alfau's novels had generated. During that period, Charlie Harris of Illinois State University was trying to lure O'Brien and the press downstate to the campus in Normal. (That was good for years of jokes: an avant-garde fiction press located in a town called *Normal*.) Harris's negotiations were dragging on—he had to not only convince the university to take us on, provide office space, etc., but also to hire O'Brien as a non-teaching professor—and at one point, when he hadn't heard from Harris in weeks, O'Brien—an impatient guy in the best of circumstances—told me he was going to call Harris and tell him to shove his offer up his ass. (His sort of language, not mine.) I advised him to call Harris and first politely ask how negotiations were going, and he was greeted with the great news that the university had just agreed to the whole deal. Again, at the risk of sounding self-congratulatory, had I not advised O'Brien to play nice, he might have scuttled our future at ISU, which would play a major role in the press's development in years to come. Had we stayed in Naperville, with none of the many benefits provided by a big university—rent-free office space, computers, health benefits, interns, an efficient postal service, a generous retirement fund, etc.—it's hard to say what would have happened.

But shortly after we arrived in Normal, Shirley and I—there were only three of us when we set up shop—noticed a personality change coming over O'Brien. Up till then he was an authority figure to his family and his students, but now, without them and being the type who needs to lord it over someone, he started becoming more arrogant—"I rarely make mistakes" he boasted in my presence—more bossy, and more unpleasant. Part of this had to do with the ugly divorce he was going through and separation from his children, part of it with his failing efforts to quit cigarettes and chocolate (I suspect he was also using Prozac), part of it with Dalkey's perpetual financial problems—the foundation money was earmarked for marketing and development, not for paying salaries and printing bills—and part of it the never-ending challenge of getting our books reviewed and stocked in stores. I stayed clear of the personal problems: I never asked about them, never wanted to discuss them over a beer after work, and in fact I was relieved that he never invited me to his new home in Normal.

There was a desperation in some of the wacky marketing schemes he started coming up with, of which this is the crown jewel:

Since we were beginning to reprint some of the modernists—we had already done Ronald Firbank and Djuna Barnes, and would eventually reprint some Gertrude Stein novels and Ford Madox Ford's *March of*

Literature—he decided we should identify and contact every American professor who had written about any of them, and then ask them to contribute $1000 toward further titles by these authors, for which their names would be listed in the back (like donors in a playbill), along with a free copy. I flat out told him that that wouldn't work, because (a) every academic I knew complained they were underpaid (including O'Brien!) and thus highly unlikely to donate $1000; and (b) other publishers didn't ask to be funded for reprints, so why were we? It might strike some as a scam. But he was adamant—once he got an *idée fixe* in his head, it was impossible to dislodge it—and so began a year-long campaign. First, we asked interns—and thank Xenu we had interns—to go through back issues of the *MLA Bibliography* to identify everyone who had written on any of those four over the previous fifteen years; then they had to locate what schools they had taught at, and verify they were still there, or track them to their current lairs; then they had to get the exact address of every one of those English departments, in many cases having to place phone calls to discover whether Prof. X taught in the English Department or some other one; then we purchased a mailing list of professors who had noted an interest in Modernism on some profile or other. Then we had to write a proposal letter—"we" meaning me: even though O'Brien knew what he wanted such letters to say, he always wanted me to write the first draft so that he would have something to criticize and revise. Then we (=me) had to write and design an insert brochure outlining our modernism plans; then we debated whether we should include a self-addressed envelope, to help the profs along; then we discussed whether they should be pre-stamped, to make it even easier for them to reply (even though most probably had free mailing privileges at their schools). We came up with a hundred or so names, and John went to work on his beloved pocket calculator ("If 30 professors donate $1000 each, that will allow us to publish three new books; if 50 come aboard . . ."). All this occupied a year's time, wore out a half-dozen interns and at least one "faculty advisor" from ISU's English department, and rang up huge bills for the phone calls, the mailing list, printing the brochures, buying the size envelope that would fit inside a normal one, maybe pre-stamping the interior ones (I forget) but definitely paying postage for the mailed ones, etc. On the day they were finally mailed out, he came into my office and said, "You know, I don't think this is going to work." I wanted to leap out of my chair and strangle him: I *told* him a *year* ago it wouldn't!! And sure enough, not a single professor sent us a check: he told me later a few said they might have contributed had it been more like $100, and others asked why were we asking for funding for reprints when other publishers didn't. (He didn't tell me if any asked if he was crazy or a scam-artist, though I'm guessing there were a few.) The majority on the mailing list simply didn't respond. And then, referring to the failed scheme a few months later, he actually said, "I still think it would work." But by then he was off on other Pollyanna marketing schemes, none of which ever worked, and then complained I never showed any interest in marketing. O'Brien remained convinced, perhaps until his dying day, that there was a magic key to unlocking hordes of new customers for our rather esoteric books if only we worked hard enough to find it.

Teased about my attitude once when a bunch of us were in New Your City for some reason—including our latest marketing manager (they came and went with the seasons)—I responded, "It's not that I don't like marketing, it's that I don't like wasting money on things that don't work." One of our succession of publicists once got mad at me for dismissing her plans to sponsor a reading in a nearby Illinois town by one of our authors, June Akers Seese (for whose slim works O'Brien had a liking that no one else understood.) She actually yelled at me, "You never want to do anything!" So I said, "OK: Do the reading, but keep track of all of your expenses and of the number of books we sell there." Result: the sales manager sheepishly admitted that she (the press) spent about $300 on the event and we sold about fifteen copies of Seese's books. Our net earnings on paperbacks were around $3 a copy, meaning the sales manager spent $300 to earn $45. Meaning we lost money, didn't make money. That was the end result of every marketing plan that O'Brien and/or the short-lived publicists and sales managers attempted, yet they still complained that I didn't like marketing. Same with ads: a few of our authors complained that we didn't take out ads for their new books, but on the rare occasion we did, there was no significant bump in sales, certainly not enough to cover the expense of the ad. Again, we lost money, didn't make it. I seemed to be the only one at Dalkey who considered that a bad business practice. "Nonprofit" is a tax classification, not a marketing strategy.

I've forgotten the names of all our publicity/sales managers—depression will do that—save one: a lovely woman named Carolyn Kuebler. She worked for us for five or six months in 1994–95, was unhappy there, left to start *Rain Taxi* later in 1995 with Randall Heath and Eric Lorberer, and eventually became editor of the *New England Review*. All of our office managers (all women) were nice, but none lasted more than a year. At some earlier point O'Brien had hired his girlfriend (and former student) Angela Weaser, who did a variety of things—sales, marketing/publicity, office management—including criticizing my cover designs.

7

Back to 1992 and Fairchild Hall, where ISU housed us. We were on the third floor, and Fiction Collective was on the first. There was some camaraderie between us, and I was able to get one of their staff to help me with creating digital images of my covers. (Previous to that, I would send the printer the photo I wanted to use, the author/title type on a separate page, then a crude, photocopied paste-up of how I wanted it to look, and they took it from there.) Harris grouped FC2 and Dalkey together as the Publishing Unit, which I had nothing to do with (and couldn't now tell you what it did). In addition to taking on interns—part of ISU's deal was that we would offer hands-on training to students interested in a publishing career—O'Brien started hiring a succession of office managers and marketing/publicity people. While he attended to them, and to dealing with his various Boards of Directors and foundation contacts, he left most of the actual editing to me. I was fine with that, but I was expected to continue to participate in most of those other activities as well (except for the Board of Directors: I met with one version of them only once, to present our forthcoming titles for that year). We were up to doing about twenty books a year by that time, so I had my hands full seeing them through the press (and three issues a year of the *Review*): copyediting and proofreading them, designing covers and writing jacket copy, sometimes soliciting blurbs, getting bound galleys and mailing them, and later finished copies, to reviewers; attending trade shows; designing and writing our semiannual catalogs and special library mailings, etc. etc.

I often had to interrupt this real work for yet another promotional scheme of O'Brien's. In 1993 he came up with the idea of printing and distributing samplers of our forthcoming titles. That entailed extra work for Shirley and me: making/editing the selections, writing headnotes for them, designing its interior and cover, typesetting the 64-page book, proofreading it, dealing with printers, mailing them out (not sure to who)—all with no discernible results. We did two issues of *A Dalkey Archive Reader* before abandoning it as yet another expensive waste of time. The cover for the first came from McElroy's *Women and Men* (see p. 55), but the second depicts Gloria Swanson at the old Roxy Theatre in New York—I can't for the life of me remember why I used that splendid photograph.

O'Brien only occasionally edited a book, and his approach was totally different than mine. I assumed authors knew what they were doing, and had reworked and revised their book until it achieved its desired final form. As an author myself, I didn't like editors messing with my prose, and assumed other authors felt likewise. I limited myself mostly to copyediting, and remember only a few occasions when I suggested that an author move a passage near the end of a book to the very end as a conclusion, or pointed out a violation of point-of-view. While I might *suggest*, O'Brien *insisted*. When he took on a manuscript—one of "his" authors, not one of "mine"—he regarded it as merely the raw materials for a publishable novel. O'Brien didn't dare make or suggest changes to Sorrentino's immaculate manuscripts, but his approach to others reminded me of something Gil said in an interview: "A friend of mine once told me that every editor he'd ever known looked at all manuscripts the same way, i.e., this is not THE manuscript, this is the PROMISE of a manuscript—the McCoy soon to emerge after EDITING!"[4] He worked extensively on June Akers Seese's manuscripts, even rewriting sentences and inserting transitional ones, but was annoyed when he learned I had mailed her the edited manuscript for approval instead of handing it over to Shirley for typesetting. He was quite proud of reducing Michael Stephens's huge manuscript of what became *The Brooklyn Book of the Dead* (1994) to a third of its original size; *Season of Coole* had been one of the very first novels O'Brien reprinted, but when

---

4 Page 99 in S. E. Gontarski's "Working at Grove: An Interview with Gilbert Sorrentino," *RCF* 10.3 (Fall 1990), an issue I especially enjoyed working on, with a cool cover that departed slightly from our usual ones.

Stephens submitted a complex, lengthy prequel to it—a five-stranded work entitled *Five Jack Coole* dealing with many generations of that outrageous Irish family—O'Brien told him he was only interested in the modern section. It was either that or nothing, Stephens felt, so he made the cuts, which O'Brien further whittled away at. He spent a lot of time getting Scott Zwiren's *God Head* into publishable shape, and convinced himself that it would be a best-seller: I overheard him telling our sales manager that he thought it could sell 30,000 copies! It was rare for one of our books to sell 3,000. *God Head* came out a few months after I left, but having read it—O'Brien asked me to vet his edited manuscript—I would be shocked if it sold more than 1500 copies. Granted, some authors at major publishers expect and even enjoy working closely with good editors, and in extreme cases (Gordon Lish vs. Raymond Carver) let them totally transform their material, but this is rare at small literary houses.

Nor did he limit himself to unpublished works: I was shocked that he wanted to correct an error (not a typo, which is acceptable, but an error in geography) in Jacques Roubaud's *The Great Fire of London*. Di Bernardi had translated the sentence exactly as Roubaud published it, but O'Brien felt free to correct it. Had he been an editor of Shakespeare, he would have "corrected" the reference in *The Winter's Tale* to the seacoast of Bohemia. A textual purist of sorts, I argued that an editor can correct an error in a manuscript, with the author's approval, but can't correct an error in a *published* book, aside from obvious typos, without the author's consent. He didn't give a fuck about authors (again, his language, not mine). I was even more disturbed when he mentioned that he had "corrected" some of Alfau's English when re-setting *Locos* in 1988—again, without telling the author.

As I said, O'Brien had changed for the worse after we arrived in Normal, and I began losing respect for him, and him for me: partly because I questioned most of marketing schemes and partly because I wasn't showing due reverence. My office was located at the end of a hall, lined with O'Brien's books—they occupied almost every open wall in the entire office[5]—and when leaving, I could turn right and exit through his large office/meeting room, and say goodbye, or exit down the hall, thus avoiding him. I began opting for the latter—since he was treating me more and more like just another employee, I treated him like the boss—which he later told me hurt him. He started finding flimsy excuses to reprimand me: in 1993 or so Shirley switched from her old, clunky digital typesetting machine to a newer model. When O'Brien saw the first issue of the *Review*

---

5 In 1995 or so, he paid a local bookseller (Babbitt's Books) to assess the value of his library, then "donated" it to Dalkey as a tax write-off.

it produced, he complained that the cover didn't look as good as previous issues, implying it was a lapse in quality control on my part. As it happens, critic Dennis Barone was visiting us for an article he was writing about us, so I set the new issue on my desk alongside the previous one and asked if he could see any difference. He spent a moment comparing them, then admitted he didn't see any difference whatsoever. So much for O'Brien's complaint. He was also miffed when he heard I didn't agree with his megalomaniac assessment that Dalkey was "the most important publisher in America," and called me into his office to ask me why. I explained that William Gaddis didn't give us his latest novel, and I assumed Thomas Pynchon wouldn't either. The conversation sputtered out after that. (One of the best literary small presses? yes; but "the most important publisher in America" was obviously an extension of his egotism.)

Around 1994 or 1995, he reprimanded me for not attending a reading given by a visiting FC2 author, and complained about my general attitude, implying I'd better shape up. So I said—appeasingly, not threateningly, or calling his bluff—"Maybe I should just quit." He instantly began back-peddling, and I later learned he suffered a panic attack that night. Since he had turned over to me nearly all the editorial duties, he realized that if I suddenly walked out, Dalkey would grind to a halt. He knew that only I knew what stages our current and forthcoming books were at—many of which he hadn't even read—or the stages of the next year of the *Review*. He was aware of how many things I was responsible for: the catalogs, arranging and attending trade shows, dealing with printers, requesting and then assigning books for review in *RCF* (as well as the ads in the back), screening the increasing number of book proposals were received every week, corresponding weekly with dozens of people (via typewriter and snail-mail; we didn't get email until mid-1996), and a number of other responsibilities I've forgotten.

Why didn't I leave? Because I didn't know what else to do with myself. Depression had smothered my so-called career, and the job *did* allow me to pursue some side interests. On weekends, if I was caught up, I'd go to the empty office and putter away at the Firbank bibliography I would later publish (see part 2 under 1996), or continue typing up my collection of Gaddis letters for an eventual edition. Too lethargic to contemplate alternatives, I stayed.

Although I had no plans to leave, and assumed I'd be at Dalkey for the rest of my life, my casual offer to quit led O'Brien to realize that I might indeed someday quit, or that he might want to replace me. Like any smart boss, he began taking precautions, shifting some of my responsibilities to others. He invited Robert McLaughlin from ISU's English department—a great guy and a Pynchon scholar—to begin assisting me with the *Review*, ostensibly to lighten my workload but actually grooming him to take it over when/if I left. Poor Bob: around this time, O'Brien asked me to write a brief history of Dalkey Archive that we could print as a brochure to send to prospective funders; I began doing so, and it was after writing a few pages that I became conscious of the decisive role I played in Dalkey's success by way of the early Markson and Alfau books. Then O'Brien wanted me to expand it to a history of small presses in America, again to demonstrate to potential funders their (our) importance in the larger cultural scheme. I told O'Brien I simply didn't have time for a project that would probably reach book-length, so he asked McLaughlin to write it instead. He spent about half a year doing so, and presented us with a 150–200 page manuscript. I speed-read through it and was very impressed, for Bob had clearly done his homework, but by then O'Brien had lost interest in the venture, or realized that few if any foundation people would actual read something that long (which I could have told him), so he set Bob's manuscript aside and nothing ever came of it.[6] Another waste of time and effort, which O'Brien had a gift for.

He also began shifting my cover design responsibilities to others. By 1995, Dalkey's staff had increased to a half-dozen full-timers, and included a part-time graphic designer named Todd Bushman, a quiet kid who kept aloft from the toxic workplace. He began to design more and more of our covers, sometimes with my input, sometimes without, and we started using some work from outside freelancers. Two spectacular examples of such contributions, far beyond what I could have created, are the covers for Wilfrido Nolledo's *But for the Lovers*, a 1970 novel that Robert Coover recommended we reprint (and for which I convinced him to write an introduction), and a collection of essays on Christine Brooke-Rose:

---

6 By un uncanny coincidence, I learned McLaughlin died on 5 September 2022 (age 65), on or about the day I typed this paragraph.

O'Brien insisted on making our tiny group more corporate: weekly meet-ings, employee rules, a big sales chart posted on the wall, and so forth. (Needless to say, the rules were for others, not for him, as I'll show in a later anecdote.) In the beginning, John, Shirley, and I were more or less equals, and treated each other as such, but by this time O'Brien had established a boss–employee hierarchy. Sensing my loss of respect for him, he started finding excuses to criticize my work. When the pictured *Utterly Other Discourse* arrived in 1995, a book I had edited—our earlier reprint of Brooke-Rose's *Amalgamemnon* was my idea—he leafed through it and then called me into his office to criticize it, saying it was poorly organized for one thing—even though it was modeled on the format *he* created for the *Review*—and poorly written, though it was clear to me that he hadn't even read it. I sat there in silence, then got up to leave, knowing that he was bullshitting and just wanted to criticize me for something, anything. More and more I sat quietly, eyes averted, when he ranted about this or that, not even bothering to respond when I knew he was talking nonsense. He took to slipping memos under my office door after I left for the day, for me to read the next morning. (An early riser, I was always the first to arrive.) In one memo he complained that I was slipping and needed to pay more attention to my work, for he had noted three typos I allowed in books over the last year (1993–94). I thought about that for a moment: during that period, we published maybe two dozen books, averaging 250-plus pages each, and three issues of the *Review* (also 250-plus pages). Lacking a little calculator like his, I got out pencil and paper and did the math: 24 books x 250 pages = 6000 pages, and 3 times 250 *RCF* pages = another 750 pages, totaling 6750 pages, then round up to 7000 for all the catalog and jacket copy I wrote. So: over the course of 7000 printed pages, I missed *only* three typos?! (I'm sure I missed more, but he mentioned only three.) At any other publisher, that would be cause for celebration, maybe even a raise. But not for O'Brien: the man who once insisted on "perfect copy" also expected perfect proofreading skills.

But here's the kicker: by 1994 we had sold out of one of O'Brien's early titles, Raymond Queneau's *Pierrot Mon Ami* (1987). (Why he left the title in French I don't know; he mocked John Updike's suggestion that it should maybe have been called "My Pal Pierrot," which I agree would have been better.) As I usually did when reprinting an older book, I reread it for typos and found 14 of them—mostly mere typos, but one in which a character's age (or name, I can't remember) was contradictory. There was a light occasion in which I mentioned this in front of a few others, and O'Brien laughed it off, pleading he was working single-handed back then. So: it was OK for him to make 14 errors in a 160-page novel, but I get reprimanded for allowing three in 7000 pages?! I was tempted to write a blistering response to his memo, but I simply left a penciled note on it and filed it for others to find later. Around this time I caught sight of a memo to the staff noting a slackening of editorial control (or some such phrase), which was untrue—no matter how dissatisfied I was becoming, I didn't let it affect my work. It became clear he wanted me out, and he was preparing the grounds for justifying doing so, even if it meant spreading lies.

Rants ignored in silence, ridiculous memos slipped under the door, baseless accusations of derelictions of duties. He once complained that I wasn't making a greater effort to find cheaper printers than we were currently using, and instanced a recent FC2 book that Curtis White told him about. (Curt was an ISU professor I had met a few times, and a talented writer—Dalkey later published several of his books. I had much more in common with him than with O'Brien. In another time, another place, we might have become friends.) So I asked for a list of the printers they used, sent each of them a request for a quote for a forthcoming book, then sent the same request with the same specs to our three regular printers. Every single one of FC2's printers came in higher than ours. When I informed O'Brien of this, he shrugged it off and mumbled something about needing to keep an eye on this. He was often rude to suppliers and distributors, suspicious they were trying to take advantage of him: around about this time, he asked me for the phone number of one of our printer contacts, and a half-hour later I received a call from the contact complaining that he had never been so insulted in all his life. On an earlier occasion, after settling a financial dispute over the phone with David Wilk of Inland Book Company, O'Brien called me into his office and confidently predicted (a) the check wouldn't arrive, (b) if it did, it would be for the wrong amount, or (c) the check would bounce. But a few days later, the check arrived for the correct amount and cleared. He loved making predictions, and never relented even though most proved wrong.

Sometime in 1995 he hired a full-time fundraiser, Barbara Something, the wife of our current full-time sales manager Joel Something, paying her $30,000 a year. (I was making $25K at the time.) During her six months there, she didn't raise a dime on her own; her only success was to follow up on a lead I gave her. I wanted to publish *The Complete Fiction of W. M. Spackman*, which I had been preparing for years and for which we had a contract, though O'Brien kept postponing its publication. (Contracts typically have a clause stating the book must be published within a specified amount of time, usually 12 to 18 months, but O'Brien ignored such clauses. If I pointed one out for a delayed book, he would fire back "Fine; we'll cancel the contract and they can take it elsewhere," or words to that effect. His needs and wishes were *always* privileged over those of others.) I told Barbara that the Spackman heirs were rich and might help underwrite the project, which is what happened, though not till after I left, and in fact I heard later that O'Brien would have canceled publication if they didn't pay up.

My departure was the result of yet another memo O'Brien slipped under my door in January 1996. It was a 10-page set of employee rules—apparently modeled on ISU's employee handbook—many of which were aimed at reducing and confining my previous responsibilities. Once his partner, it was clear he wanted me to be merely an employee, an obsequious yes-man who wouldn't challenge his ever-changing, often contradictory decisions. I read about halfway through it, set it aside, typed a brief letter of resignation—in full corporate mode by this point, O'Brien wanted everything in writing—walked into his office and handed it to him. He read it over and looked up to say, "I figured this was how you would respond," implying that his new rules were indeed designed to push me out. He asked for some time to process it, then (later that day or the next) asked if I would be willing to stay until the end of the fiscal year, June 20th, six months off. I agreed for two reasons: the first was I had no plans for what I would do next; the second and more important was that I was deeply concerned about the fates of four or five forthcoming books, and feared Dalkey would screw them up, if not cancel them.

Knowing I would soon be leaving was an immense relief, allowing me to sit back and watch with detachment O'Brien's subsequent antics. At our weekly meetings, O'Brien would announce new plans and procedures that afterward would cause us to roll our eyes at each other as we returned to our offices. He was so obsessed with funding that he proposed making it a rule that every new book had to be funded by someone or other: a foreign ministry, a foundation, a university if the author taught at one, and as a last resort, even the author. No more free rides. He didn't pursue this policy, but for unsupported authors he hit upon the idea of a number of series named after benefactors. Want to become one? go to https://www. dalkeyarchive.com/giving/funding-a-named-series/.

I wasn't the only one who had lost respect for him by this time. In late May or early June, Shirley Geever quit, his long-time employee and confidante; she was his department secretary even before O'Brien started the *Review*, and knew him better than anyone. In her resignation letter, of which I only caught a glimpse, she accused him of becoming "a real rat-bastard" in recent years, for he had taken to criticizing her in the same demeaning terms he had been using with me, and making equally baseless accusations, for Shirley was perhaps the most efficient, reliable person I ever worked with. I loved working with her, even though she didn't love our books. She quickly found a job at one of Bloomington-Normal's many insurance companies.

8

My final clash with O'Brien came along about this time. Shirley had just finished preparing for the printer the summer issue of the *Review*, "New Finnish Fiction." O'Brien was doing more and more all-translation issues—we had already done the French, Italians, Danes, and Flemings—underwritten by foreign governments of course, though such issues were not what subscribers originally signed up for. As I said, we had a big sales chart on the wall, fairly useless for comparative purposes, for it was a bar graph of sales for every book we had ever published, mixing recent books with those that had been selling for years. He had probably seen one in a movie and figured that's what businessmen did. He loved using his calculator to analyze sales trends, etc.—with earth-shattering findings such as novels sold better than poetry—though I could tell he didn't even know the difference between mean and median averages. Around about April he wrote a large message on the chart stating that new books were not to be sent to the printer without his permission—unnecessary, because I was the only one who dealt with the printers. Assuming that mandate applied only to books, not to the *Review*, which, he told me when I first started, was on a very fixed schedule: if issues didn't arrive when expected (February, June, October), impatient subscribers would write in to complain. But when O'Brien learned I had sent the summer issue off, he called the printer and told them to mail the package back by overnight mail (very expensive: we were still pre-digital, so the package consisted of hardcopy pages and the mechanicals for the cover, images, and ads). He left the package sitting on the edge his desk for all to see for three or four days, and then authorized its shipment to the printer (again by overnight mail). He merely wanted to exert his power, to show everyone who was boss, yet this ultimately provided another example of cutting off his nose to spite his face. By the time the finished copies came back from the printer—he actually praised me for its cover design, much to my surprise—the elevator had broken down, and without the elevator the 2000 or so individually packaged issues could not be taken down to the post office for weeks. The issue reached subscribers a month late, and I bet there were letters.

I barely spoke at all with O'Brien during the final month—I sat in silence the day he came into my office to explain why he wanted to postpone the Spackman, again, though he had plenty of room on the schedule for "his" books, like the William Eastlake trilogy I had just finished preparing, and the reprints of Philip Wylie's *Generation of Vipers* and two Aldous

Huxley novels I had prepped for the printer. (He boasted of sending the Huxley Estate a big check for four of his novels, so big that Dalkey wouldn't have to send them royalties for years; I was tempted to explain him that all did was to allow *them* to earn interest on a big chunk of money that could have been Dalkey's had he licensed the novels one at a time.) I looked away as he blathered, remaining passive-aggressively silent until he finished and left the room. During those final months, my office was across the hall and elevator from the main office, which suited me fine.

In another letter slipped under my door, he pointed out that, as I packed my stuff, I had to leave behind the manuscript of *Chromos* that Alfau had gifted me with (me, not the press) and leave behind any books I reviewed for *RCF*—he specified the bound galley of Gass's *Tunnel*—even though it's a universal practice for a reviewer to keep the book he reviews. Universal practices and procedures were for others, not for John O'Brien, who displayed what would later be called a Trumpian attitude of exceptionalism. I spent most of my final day alone in my office—as with Carolyn Kuebler a year and a half earlier, he insisted that employees work their full shift on their last day, even if it meant fiddling their thumbs in an empty office—though at one point he wandered in to ask if I need any help moving stuff. (I didn't own a car in all the years I worked at Dalkey. Dave Wallace was astonished at this, and offered to give me a ride if I ever needed one.) I said no. I pointed to the shelf where the finished materials for the next half-dozen books were—and I think most if not all of the Fall 1996 *RCF*—and told him he could call me if he had any questions about them. (He never did.) When four o'clock came, I walked out the door without saying goodbye. No going-away party, needless to say. A little later, I walked to the supermarket to buy a bottle of champagne, where I ran into Curt White. Smiling at him for the first time, I told him I was off to celebrate.

Two weeks after I left O'Brien called to tell me about some mail I had received—I stopped by the next day to pick it up at the front desk, avoiding him—and that's the last I ever heard from him.[7]

Shirley was gone, Joel and Barbara left (or were fired) shortly after I left, and then this happened: At one of our group meetings a few months earlier, O'Brien announced that employees would not be allowed to take vacations; unlike almost every other publisher—indeed unlike almost every company—O'Brien argued that everyone had to be available at all times in case an emergency occurred, such as the *New York Times* calling

---

7 In 2013 I published *The Letters of William Gaddis* with Dalkey—the Estate's choice, not mine—but I dealt only with Jeremy Davies, not O'Brien, which is the way I wanted it.

for either a review copy or an author's photo, or a foundation inviting us to submit a grant proposal. I think those were the only two examples he gave, both of which are bogus. Anyone in the office could send someone a review copy, and everyone knew that I had an index card box on my desk containing photos of most of our authors. And O'Brien's fearful fantasy that some foundation would call him and say they have some leftover money to dispose of as long as he could submit a grant within 24 hours was just that, a fantasy. Truth is, nothing had ever happened that required all hands on deck. Sitting there listening to this nonsense, I just smiled, for I never took vacations anyway (nor did Shirley, I believe). But mark the sequel:

By August 1996, the staff was back down to three: John, Angela, and a young office manager named Stacy Klein. At that point, when vacations would indeed have been impractical, O'Brien decided . . . wait for it . . . to take a week's vacation with Angela, in utter disregard of his own policy! Stacy was left alone in the office, and then got a panicked call from *Publishers Weekly* complaining they hadn't yet received the full-page ad Dalkey had reserved for their Fall Announcements issue. (A waste of money for all but the largest publishers, but I digress.) Stacy didn't know anything about it, and told *PW* she would try to contact John or Angela. They were up in woods of Wisconsin, and when she finally reached them, Angela said they had changed their mind about the ad. When Stacy conveyed this to the *PW* guy, he freaked, for the page had already been set aside for them, and the issue couldn't repaginated. (I can't remember the technical details that Stacy later told me about.) So once again she had to make several calls to the vacationers, who reiterated they weren't interested, then relayed that to *PW*, who offered a discount on the ad, or a payment plan, which they accepted. So the one time all hands needed to be on deck, O'Brien and Angela had abandoned ship. Stacy left sometime after that, but not before telling me one more outrageous story. For that one, see part 2 under "David Markson, *Reader's Block* (1996)."

When I left, I had no plans, no idea what to do with myself other than to return to Colorado. I certainly didn't want to stay in publishing, nor did it even occur to me to try again to find a teaching position somewhere. I had always assumed I'd be working at Dalkey for the rest of my life, so at age 45 I had to start all over. But it all worked out for the best: a former bookseller, I soon went to work for Borders Books & Music—first in a suburban Denver store, then in their home office in Ann Arbor, where I've lived ever since—which not only provided a saner, more enjoyable work environment, but also provided the conditions under which I could write my huge history of the novel, something I never could have done had I remained at Dalkey. Contrary to F. Scott Fitzgerald, there are second acts in American life.

9

I want to conclude with some random things I enjoyed during my Dalkey days, but first, let me go on record as saying I'm grateful to John O'Brien, even though he was a horrible example of a human being: arrogant, egotistic, vindictive, dishonest—in addition to his habitual lying, Shirley implied he "cooked the books"—condescending, hypocritical, captious, obstinate, maddeningly inconsistent and contradictory, hard-nosed but sometimes naively optimistic, insulting, thin-skinned and quick to take offense when unintended, nepotistic, neurotic—he dragged me along to many foundation meetings, at great expense, because he hated to fly alone, and he couldn't go anywhere without his safety-blanket briefcase, even to restaurants—and given to mindless exaggerations: any review we received was either a rave or a pan, things were either the best or worst, exactly or nothing like, perfect or "deeply flawed," etc. *But*, he gave me a job when I desperately needed one, arranged for me to teach a few writing courses at Illinois Benedictine to supplement my income, gave me unasked-for raises periodically, and let me publish almost anything I wanted to. After we moved to ISU, he even offered to set me up with a lady professor in the English department, though I was still too depressed for dating.

Although I didn't particularly like to travel, I was able to visit some major cities for the first time—Chicago of course, then San Francisco, Washington DC, Dallas, Toronto, Los Angeles, San Diego—and always enjoyed any opportunity to go back to New York City, mostly so that I could spend downtime in its fabulous record stores. Though unsociable, I did meet some distinguished authors who had only been names before (William H. Gass, Gilbert Sorrentino, Harry Mathews, Joseph McElroy, Paul West, Marguerite Young). I danced with Mary Caponegro in a Toronto nightclub in 1993, shared a cab in New York with Nicholas Mosley (who was delighted when I told him *Judith* was my favorite novel in his Catastrophe Practice series), and talked on the phone with John Barth, Robert Coover, and Bill Vollmann. I met many of the authors I edited, as well as assorted critics. It was because of my reviews in *RCF* that Michael Dirda asked me to start reviewing books for the *Washington Post* (some 75 reviews to date) and my appearances there led to other assignments from the *Chicago Tribune* and *Los Angeles Times*. As the book review editor of *RCF* I could request books from anywhere, which certainly saved me a small fortune over the years.

More of a scholar than a book publisher, I enjoyed editing the *Review*: as I said earlier, at least half of the issues published between 1987 and

1996 were on authors I proposed, beginning with Chandler Brossard, followed by Joseph McElroy, David Markson, John Barth, Alexander Theroux, Paul West, William H. Gass, Jerome Charyn, Felipe Alfau, Djuna Barnes, Stanley Elkin, and Brigid Brophy. (The latter two died just around the time their issues appeared.[8]) A few weeks after I left Dalkey, I was invited by Charlie Harris's wife Victoria to contribute an essay to a forthcoming issue on Carole Maso, which appeared in Fall 1997—my last essay for the *Review*.

The most fun issue I worked on was our "Younger Writers Issue" (Summer 1993). In 1992 Larry McCaffery was interviewing a number of younger writers for a forthcoming book, published in 1995 as *Some Other Frequency: Interviews with Innovative American Authors*, and proposed featuring some of them in special issue. I liked the idea, got it OK'd by O'Brien, and told Larry that we had room for three authors. Which three? We immediately agreed on William T. Vollmann and David Foster Wallace, each of whom had only published a few books by that point, but it was obvious to both of us that they were on their way to historical importance. For the third, Larry proposed Richard Powers, who I likewise loved, but I suspected we'd get criticized for featuring three white guys. At ISU, we were already getting blowback from the politically correct members of the English Department. Shortly after we arrived, we placed our Fall 1993 catalogue in their mail slots, with Edward Gorey's erotic drawing for *The Lollipop Trollops* on the cover (see p. 52), which got some knickers in a twist. I suggested Susan Daitch, whose first two novels I really liked, as well as the few short stories of hers I'd seen. Larry wasn't as familiar with her, but agreed to it. (Powers eventually got his special issue in 1998, paired with Rikki Ducornet.)

Our format called for (a) a new piece of fiction by the author, (b) an essay, preferably on a literary topic, and (c) an interview, along with critical essays on the author. Off he went to interview them—his interview with Wallace has become legendary—and over the next sixth months rounded up and sent me a number of unedited essays on them. It was my responsibility to get the new fiction and essay from our featured writers. Daitch and Vollmann were easy; the latter sent me a chapter from his forthcoming novel *The Rifles*, which entailed sending our typesetter a digital file for Intuit letters. David sent me several selections from *Infinite Jest*, and was disappointed when I told him I could only use one. (He drew a frowny face on my note when returning it to me.) For an essay, he

---

8 Coover, Don DeLillo, Guy Davenport, and Philip Roth declined my invitations to be subjects of a special issue.

offered a long one that *Harper's* had just turned down entitled "E Unibus Pluram: Television and U.S. Fiction," saying I could have it for free as long as I printed the entire thing without cuts, which I was happy to do after reading that stunning piece, which has likewise become iconic. All that was left was Larry's introduction to the issue, which he kept postponing. When I warned him that a hard deadline was fast approaching, he spent a weekend freeballing a ten-page screed that he faxed me, which I told him was unusable. So he wrote a single-paragraph foreword, Shirley printed out the entire issue, and off it went to the printer, to become one of our most popular issues, and now a collector's item.

And it was thanks to the *Review* that I became acquainted with David Foster Wallace in the first place, first as a contributor to *RCF*—I solicited two of his earliest published essays—then as a fellow Normalite, when he moved there in the summer of 1993. I didn't see him often—again, too depressed to socialize—but he would occasionally visit me at the office, looking more like a grungy grad student than a professor as he slouched in a chair, and allowed me to read his working draft of *Infinite Jest*, a tale I've sold elsewhere (*My Back Pages*, 684–712). While that book was working its way through the press, he and I edited "The Future of Fiction" issue of *RCF* that appeared around the time *Infinite Jest* came out, and which included my rave review of that magnum opus. Around 50% of the contributors were Dave's invitees, and 50% mine and O'Brien's, who contributed an essay as well. After the issue appeared—with one of my favorite authors, Karen Elizabeth Gordon, as our cover girl—O'Brien took umbrage at Dave's remark in his brief introduction that he found only three-fourths of the essays interesting, maybe suspecting his essay belonged to the other fourth. He handed me a mock letter to the editor criticizing the intro, and signed it "Don Gately" (a character in *Infinite Jest*, which he may have got from my review; I don't remember him saying he actually read the novel). I ignored it, and when the summer issue came out, he asked why I didn't include it and I pretended I thought he was just joking. (By that time I had learned when to dodge the truth.) Thanks to Dave's involvement, "The Future of Fiction" was a popular issue and eventually sold out; years later, when Dalkey reprinted it, they replaced my eye-catching cover, printed in sky blue, with a dreary one that you can look up online.

THE FUTURE OF FICTION

A Forum Edited by David Foster Wallace

Essays by Sven Birkerts, Mary Caponegro, Jonathan Franzen, Janice Galloway,
Carole Maso, Bradford Morrow, William T. Vollmann, Curtis White, and others

THE REVIEW OF CONTEMPORARY FICTION

SPRING 1996 • EIGHT DOLLARS

10

But my fondest memory might be walking home after work on late Tuesday afternoons. I would cross the beautiful campus to E. College Street—Normal's three-block Main Street—to the independent record store near the corner of S. Linden, for Tuesday was new releases day. I would scan the wall of new stuff, usually picked out one or two, then looked through the bins for any intriguing used CDs that may have arrived since my last visit (especially trip-hop and female-fronted bands). Then I would take my catch next door to a small Mexican restaurant that offered "Burritos As Big As Your Head." Seating myself with one of those and a Pepsi, I would tear off the shrinkwrap and pore over the CD booklets. Comfortably stuffed, I would then cross the railroad tracks and walk to my basement apartment at 404 E. Vernon Avenue, change, and listen to the CDs I had bought that day. Then I went to work on whatever manuscript I had brought home.

PART 2
My Dalkey Archive Books

At Lauren Fairbanks's *Muzzle Thyself* reading, Summer 1991

BELOW ARE ALL the books I either suggested, acquired, or solicited. I always ran them by O'Brien first, for he's the one who signed the contracts. In all my years, he turned down only two of my suggestions, one at the beginning, and one at the end. A fan of William T. Vollmann from his first book on, I asked around 1990 if he had a small-press type book that his major publishers wouldn't be interested in, and he sent me a manuscript entitled *Wordcraft: Hints and Notes*, a writing guide using passages from his own works as examples (including the in-progress *Fathers and Crows*). I liked it but O'Brien didn't, mostly because of what he criticized as Vollmann's attitude. Given how popular Vollmann later became, I'm sure we would have done well with it, though the fact that Vollmann has never published the book suggests he has had second thoughts about it. I mailed the manuscript back to Bill, and regret that I didn't make a copy first. In early 1996, the year I left, Mary Caponegro submitted a dazzling short story sequence called *Five Doubts*; I told Mary I very much wanted to do it, but the boss adamantly rejected it: "I will not publish this book!" he declaimed in a memo. Upon its publication two years later by Marsilio, it was very favorably reviewed in the *Review of Contemporary Fiction* by Bob McLaughlin, my replacement.

Following the first part of this list, there is a section on fence-straddlers: books that O'Brien acquired but turned over to me, which sort of became "my" books as a result. And following that is a short section on books reprinted in the years following my departure that I probably had something to do with, as I'll explain. In part 3 of this book I go into a more detail on certain authors who needed a little more space.

And I might point out that, despite O'Brien's widely publicized claim in the early days that he would keep all of Dalkey's titles permanently in print, he failed to reprint quite a few of "mine" after they sold out, and even some of "his" in later years.

§

David Markson, *Wittgenstein's Mistress* (1988), discussed in part 1. Two years later, I wrote about the novel in an essay for *RCF*'s John Barth/ David Markson number (Summer 1990), which became the basis for my afterword added to fourth paperback printing (1995), which I resented: O'Brien asked me to write it merely as a marketing ploy to resell the novel to booksellers. (He did this often in later years; when stock ran low on a title that he wanted to keep in print, he would give it a new ISBN and advertise it as "back in print.") In the March 2012 printing, he replaced my afterword with a long essay David Foster Wallace had written for the same special issue.

Felipe Alfau, *Locos: A Comedy of Gestures* (1988, Afterword by Mary McCarthy). Thereby hangs a tale: see part 1, and then part 3 for more on Alfau.

Alan Ansen, *Contact Highs: Selected Poems* (1989, Introduction by SM). I had prepared this a few years earlier for Beat-oriented Water Row Press, which had published a few chapbooks by Ansen—an old friend of William Gaddis, which is how I got to know him—but after the publisher changed his mind, I asked O'Brien if Dalkey could do it, which he reluctantly agreed to; Dalkey hadn't done any poetry books until then, and would do very few in the future, but O'Brien did have some interest in Beat writers. For the cover, at my request Allen Ginsberg sent me a newly captioned print of a famous photo of his featuring Ansen and other Beats. Like Dalkey's earliest books, this was a split edition: about 200 or 300 hardbacks for collectors and libraries, maybe 700 paperbacks for the trade.

Edward Dahlberg, *Samuel Beckett's Wake and Other Uncollected Prose* (1989, Introduction by SM). Compiled at Rutgers while I was going through a Dahlberg phase, and fortunately O'Brien liked him well enough to accept it: at 343 pages, it was the longest book Dalkey had done. When I submitted the index, I neglected to tell Shirley Geever to set it in two columns, assuming she knew that, but Dalkey had never done an indexed book before, so she set it in one column. I learned to be more specific. Some of our interns later made fun of Dahlberg's bleary cover image (see p. 17).

Clifford S. Mead, *Thomas Pynchon: A Bibliography of Primary and Secondary Materials* (1989). Another pet project of mine; I don't know how I talked O'Brien into this. I'd known Cliff since 1982, when he sent me a flattering letter about my *Reader's Guide* to Gaddis's *Recognitions*. We kept in touch and visited each other a few times, and over the years he mailed me various iterations of this bibliography. When O'Brien OK'd publication, Cliff sent me a stack of photos to accompany the text—mostly Pynchon book covers, as well as images from his high school yearbook—and I spent many hours designing the book. In the appendix we included some of Pynchon's high school newspaper stories, which had either never been copyrighted or were in the Public Domain by then; another writer might have made a fuss and drawn attention to the matter, but Pynchon, being the smart guy he is, stayed mum. It was priced at $30 when the rest of our books were $20, so even though it sold slowly, each sale was equivalent to a book and a half. I wish we had waited a little longer, for the following year Pynchon published a new novel. A few years later, Cliff met O'Brien at a trade show in Dallas we were all attending, and took a dislike to him, describing him as "predatory."

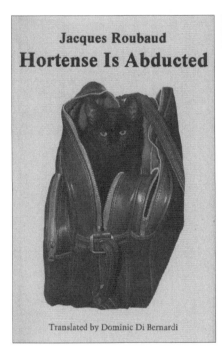

Jacques Roubaud, *Hortense Is Abducted* (1989). My favorite contribution to *RCF*'s "New French Fiction" issue was a selection from this sequel to *La belle Hortense*, translated and published by Overlook Press as *Our Beautiful Heroine* (1987). Given my enthusiasm, O'Brien told Dominic Di Bernardi (his French fiction advisor and frequent translator) to obtain rights and translate the rest, which he did quickly, for by the time the issue came out, we were able to advertise *Hortense* facing the contents page. I loved working on it, and—armed with the French original and a French dictionary—I was even able to convert into rhymed verse a recipe-poem in chapter 35 that Dom had left in prose. The comic novel features a black cat named Hotello, so for the cover I used a photo my father had taken in 1991 of my bookstore cat, Montague (named after demonologist Montague Summers), who had leaped into my father's camera bag. Keeping it all in the family, the cover for a later Roubaud novel we did, *The Princess Hoppy, or, The Tale of Labrador*, features my niece Maggie dressed up as a princess, accompanied by a neighborhood dog named Forbes, and taken by my brother Randy. (As I said in part 1, there were some things I liked about working at Dalkey.)

William H. Gass, *Willie Masters' Lonesome Wife* (1989). I fell under Gass's spell in 1979 when I read a selection from his long-in-progress novel *The Tunnel* in an eye-opening anthology entitled *In the Wake of the "Wake"* (University of Wisconsin Press), where I learned of many future favorites. I mean, look at that line-up:

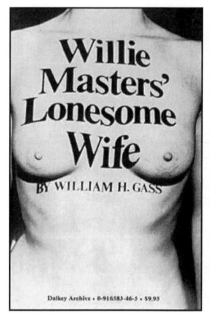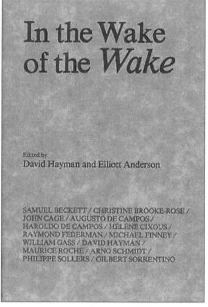

I then sought out his earlier works, including this dazzling novella, and thereafter followed his progress on *The Tunnel* in various journals and in limited editions that I couldn't really afford. Knowing *Willie Masters* was out-of-print, I pitched it while still at Rutgers to O'Brien, who agreed Gass would be a good name to add to his list. I warned him that it would be a tricky production job, but he assured me that Shirley could handle it. I mailed him my copy of the original *TriQuarterly Supplement* version (1968), and after he received it, he wrote back "I forgot, I forgot!," which aroused my suspicion that he had never read it—for anyone who has can't forget its layout. After he had obtained rights and I moved out to Illinois, we contacted *TriQuarterly* to see if they still had the layouts from which the book was created; miraculously they did, and even more miraculously they mailed a package of all the materials to us. It included pasted-up pages, with some lines of type beginning to fall off, along with all sorts of background material: a copy of the contract with the model (whose name I once wrote down but lost), outtakes and contact sheets, etc. After I repaired the layouts, we had to decide whether we were going to imitate the *TriQuarterly* original—in which each section is printed on different colored paper (blue, olive green, red, white)—or imitate the Knopf hardback edition of 1971, all in black and white. For cost reasons, O'Brien preferred the latter, so I called Gass—his wife Mary answered, and I was so afraid I was, like the person from Porlock, interrupting Gass in the rapture of composition—and asked him if he minded if we printed it in black and white. He didn't mind, and even seemed rather dismissive of it, as in It's just a bagatelle, do what you want with it. The front cover was modified from *TriQuarterly*'s.

That was the beginning of Dalkey's long relationship with Gass. As I said in part 1, he was one of the judges for the 1990 National Book Awards; I met him at the March 14th ceremony (the first and last time I wore a tuxedo) and was even seated at a table next to him. All I remember discussing was our mutual admiration for Severo Sarduy's *Cobra*, which I later reprinted (1995). Just before the fiction winner was announced, he leaned over and whispered, "I did my best." The following year *RCF* did half an issue on him, guest-edited by Arthur M. Saltzman, and I remember being terrified at copyediting Gass's fiction and nonfiction submissions; the latter was called "Simplicities," and as I started I instinctively replaced a few of his "which"s with "that"s, but then went back and erased them. I'm sure he knew the which/that rule, and if he preferred the old-fashioned "which," I wasn't going to override him, of all people. He wrote the foreword to our 1995 reprint of Stein's *Making of Americans*, which he later said was awful.

We came close to publishing *The Tunnel*; it had been under contract to Ticknor and Fields, but when he finished in 1993 or so, they decided against it. When I heard this, I asked O'Brien if we could do it, he said yes, so I contacted Gass and asked him to let us do it. His agent sent me the huge manuscript, along with a lengthy set of design and typesetting instructions, but shortly after I learned that Knopf had taken it on. On the one hand that was for the best, for the manuscript presented many technical challenges, and Knopf had far superior marketing forces. (They sent me a bound galley, which I reviewed in our Spring 1995 issue.) On the other, they didn't follow all of Gass's instructions, as I would have, and let it go out of print a few years later. In fact I remember Gass saying later he wished he had let us do it in the first place. Dalkey snapped it up and issued a paperback edition in 1999, and even an audiobook in 2006. After I left, Dalkey continued to reprint many of Gass's superb books.

Felipe Alfau, *Chromos* (1990). Alfau wrote *Locos* for money to support his family, but began writing his second novel in 1946 for his own amusement—"like building a ship in a bottle," I was once reported as saying.[1] But after he finished in 1948, he couldn't find a publisher, despite the help of writer-friends like Chandler Brossard who showed it to editors. Alfau put it in a drawer, where it stayed until 1989: again, see part 3. But I don't mention there how much trouble I had finding a suitable cover image. I even went to a photograph agency in Manhattan that had files of prints on every subject on earth. I pulled out the thick one on Spain and spent an hour going through it, but *nada*. I couldn't find any actual examples of *cromos* (Spanish chromolithographs), and finally had to settle for a photo evoking time past that I found in some book, which was too washed-out to be effective.

Patrick Grainville, *The Cave of Heaven* (1990). My second favorite contribution to *RCF*'s "New French Fiction" issue was this novel about the mysterious and erotic doings around a French excavation site, a prehistoric cave that attracts an exotic range of visitors, including a motorcycle gang. I was attracted to Grainville's excessive, imagistic prose; at the time, he was a "well-regarded and somewhat controversial French author" (as *Library Journal* noted in its positive review), but it looks like this is the only one of his many novels to have been translated into English. I couldn't figure out how to create the cover art I wanted—a cave-painting rendition of a motorcycle—so had to settle for a photograph I took of a ballerina figurine I owned against my living-room window.

Louis Zukofsky, *Collected Fiction* (1990). I liked Zukofsky' short musical novel *Little* (1970), and suggested joining to it with his earlier short story collection *It was* (1961) for a collected edition. O'Brien agreed, as did Louis's son Paul, who wrote an afterword for it. A professional violinist visiting Chicago for a concert, he invited me to dinner at the legendary Drake Hotel to discuss the project, and gave me one of his LPs. We decided to offset the longer *Little* and reset the stories in the same font, Bodoni Book, a digitized version of which Shirley had

---

1 I was reminded of this remark by a deeply informative article about Dalkey's early days, Paul Moberg's "Little House in the Suburbs," *Chicago Reader*, 2 May 1991: https://chicagoreader.com/news-politics/little-house-in-the-suburbs/. Another informative article for the historian is Lynda Stephenson's "A Storybook Beginning," *Chicago Tribune*, 1 September 1991: https://www.chicagotribune.com/news/ct-xpm-1991-09-01-9103050632-story.html. And while I'm down here providing sources for further reading, check out Dennis Barone's "What's in a Name? The Dalkey Archive Press," *Critique* 37.3 (Spring 1996): 222–39.

on her typesetting machine. But the ink was a little low the day she printed it out, and when the finished book arrived at our office, the type for *It was* was noticeably lighter, and O'Brien threw a fit. "It doesn't look anything like the first part!" he stormed over the phone. Not a little light, but *nothing* like the first part, even though, as I patiently explained, it was set in the exact same font and point size, and had been approved by Paul. That's when I learned he misused language for emphasis (as noted in part 1), and I took further judgments with a grain of salt. When Dalkey reset the book for a new edition in 1997, they made matters worse by setting the front matter and last part of the book in what looks like Times Roman, which "doesn't look anything like" Bodoni.

David Markson, *Springer's Progress* (1990). Given the success of *Wittgenstein's Mistress*, I had no trouble convincing O'Brien to reprint this 1977 novel, the funniest, cleverest thing he ever wrote. Simultaneously we published the John Barth/David Markson issue of the *Review*, which contained a few essays on *Springer*—horizontal integration. I wanted to rush both into print because Markson told me he felt mortally ill and might not be around much longer, which happily proved untrue: the hypochondriac lived for another twenty years. Because the novel was obviously autobiographical, I asked to put a 1977 photo of him on the cover. I did likewise with his *Collected Poems* a few years later, once again evoking New Directions titles from the 1950s.

Ronald Firbank, *Complete Short Stories* (1990, Textual Notes by SM).
I had been a Firbank fan ever since the 1970s; O'Brien too had read
him—and even taught one of his novels at Illinois Benedictine—and
so allowed me to prepare this collection. Only eight of the seventeen
pieces gathered here were published in Firbank's lifetime; the rest were
culled from limited editions published in the 1960s and 1970s, and
from university libraries and private collectors—one of whom was Barry
Humphries, aka Dame Edna Everage, the famous transvestite actor.

Djuna Barnes, *Ryder* (1990, Afterword by Paul West). I had admired
Barnes for years, and when granted permission by the Authors League
(her literary executors) to reprint this 1928 novel, I took the opportunity to reset the book for a more modern look and to supplement
its original illustrations with a half-dozen others that the original
publisher wouldn't allow. Knowing Paul West to be a fan of purple
prose, I asked him to furnish an afterword. This edition sold well: we
needed to reprint it only a year and a half after the first printing, and
it has gone through further printings (and cover changes) since then.

Julián Ríos, *Larva: Midsummer Night's Babel* (1990). Translator Richard
Alan Francis and one other person approached O'Brien and me at a
convention in 1989, and asked if we would like to publish what some
had called the Spanish *Ulysses*. (Yes, please!) It was a 585-page novel
in punning Joycean prose consisting of a main text on the recto pages
and editorial commentary on the versos, followed by a hundred pages
of vignettes called "Pillow Notes," a photo gallery, and an index of
names—*plus* a two-color fold-out map of London. Ríos had signed
a contract with publisher George Braziller, who intended to hire the
eminent translator Suzanne Jill Levine, but she asked for too much
money, and the contract expired. (Her name would remain on the
title page, but it's unclear how much she actually contributed.[2]) Rick
Francis had obtained a Fulbright grant to work in Madrid with the
multilingual author, and his associate said they had mucho funding
from the Spanish Ministry of Culture, so O'Brien agreed. He had
published something by Ríos in an earlier issue of *RCF*, and the novel
sounded right up our alley. When the huge manuscript arrived, O'Brien
turned it over to me and I handled the copyediting, proofreading,
etc. I don't remember him actually reading the novel, or discussing
the contents with me, which is why I'm claiming it as one of mine.
Julián shares my suspicion that he never read it.

---

2 See her "Afterwords on Afterthoughts," *RCF* 10.3 (Fall 1990): 181–82, in a
subsection of the Grove Press number on the forthcoming *Larva* (179–88).

Shirley and I had our work cut out for us. We followed the format of the Spanish original (Ediciones del Mall, 1983), but she had to typeset the recto pages first, and then go back and do the facing verso pages so that we could align the commentary. There were other typographic challenges as well: flip through the book and you'll see what I mean. We were able to improve on the original's photo gallery because Julián sent us a better set of prints, and I re-did the index. We retained the striking cover art of Antonio Saura, and stuffed the back cover with blurbs from *todo el mundo*. Printing the book was another challenge, for Quartet Books in England wanted to co-publish it with us, which meant I had to design two slightly different covers and copyright pages. The printers, McNaughton & Gunn, did a magnificent job with the book, but forgot to send Quartet their portion of the books until I reminded them, irritating the Brits to no end, and quite rightly so. The novel received a number of good reviews, especially from Michael Dirda in the *Washington Post*, but not a much-desired review from the all-important *New York Times Book Review*, despite a visit I paid to Rebecca Sinkler in late November 1990 to talk it up, and the special pleading of Carlos Fuentes. (For my clash with the *Voice Literary Supplement*, see p. 25 of the first volume of my novel history.) I was in New York beseeching Sinkler because Julián had flown over for a mini-publicity tour: he appeared at a few sparsely attended readings and events, and was the guest of honor at a party thrown for him by the late Barbara Probst Solomon at her lavish Upper East Side apartment. One evening I joined him and Rick Francis at a Greenwich Village café, along with novelist Frederic Tuten, whose last novel I had conveniently reviewed (*RCF* Fall 1988).

Six years later I published a similar but much shorter Ríos novel called *Poundemonium* (see below). The hardcover *Larva* eventually sold out, but Julián had to pressure O'Brien to publish a paperback edition, which finally appeared in 2005 with a less-striking cover.

[All the books we published in 1991 were O'Brien's; but while working on his—copyediting, cover-designing—I was also preparing a boatload of "mine" for the following year:]

Chandler Brossard, *As the Wolf Howls at My Door* (1992). I had become interested in Brossard in 1983, and when I met him I learned that he had a huge unpublished novel that he had finished a few years earlier, similar to *Wake Up. We're Almost There* (1971), his most ambitious, far-ranging novel. He had had the first 150 pages or so professionally typed, but gave up at that point, convinced no one would publish it. I offered to resume where the typist had left off, so after he typed up the rest of the handwritten manuscript, I spent weeks in the summer of 1984 preparing a professional-looking submission copy. I tried and failed to interest the few publishers I approached in the mid-1980s, so after I joined Dalkey I convinced O'Brien to take it on. He even used portions of the manuscript for a class in copyediting he was teaching at Illinois Benedictine. The 466-page novel was published in April 1992, with cover art supplied by Chandler, and flatteringly dedicated to me. It didn't do well, but I'm glad I got his last novel into print while he was still alive. It went o.p. early in this century, but fortunately Rick Harsch reprinted it in 2021 with a spirited introduction by Zachary Tanner, along with several other Brossard novels.[3]

After *As the Wolf Howls* came out, I proposed publishing an omnibus of Chandler's shorter works, which he enthusiastically supported, even supplying a title for the collection, but he died the following year. O'Brien initially agreed to the project and Shirley typeset it, but after I left in 1996 he abandoned it. It wouldn't be published until 2005, under the title Chandler had chosen a dozen years earlier: *Over the Rainbow? Hardly: Collected Short Seizures* (Sun Dog Press), which got a full-page review in the *New York Times Book Review*.

Rikki Ducornet, *The Fountains of Neptune* (1992). When a package of Ducornet's manuscripts arrived at the Naperville office in 1991, O'Brien turned it over to me to evaluate; I reacted so enthusiastically

---

3 Visit https://coronasamizdat.com/index.php.

that she became one of "my" authors for the next four years: see part 3 for the full story.

Timothy d'Arch Smith, *Alembic* (1992). I'd known of this British biblio-phile for years because of his writings on Montague Summers, but didn't know he had written a novel until my friend Maurice Cloud, who had been in touch him for a while, suggested that d'Arch Smith send it to me, after failing to find a British publisher. Carefully typewritten, it required little more than closing up some words (e.g., spreadeagled for spread-eagled), which he approvingly found "Joycean."A friend of the author's designed the striking cover, and I was able to elicit a strong blurb from Alexander Theroux. D'Arch Smith, a bookseller and collector who specialized in the occult—Jimmy Page was one of his steady customers, and the novel features a band clearly modeled on Led Zeppelin—was especially happy with the bookbinding, saying it was far better than any British publisher could have done.

René Crevel, *Putting My Foot in It* (1992). A 1933 surrealist novel with quite a production team: a foreword by Ezra Pound (from a 1939 essay on the French writer), an introduction by poet Édouard Roditi (who died just after submitting it), a translation by Thomas Buckley with lots of input from David Rattray, who was going to translate Crevel's *Etes-vous fous?* for us but died suddenly at the age of 57 (as his widow informed me when I inquired in 1993 about his progress), and with cover art by the fabulous Rikki Ducornet. Buckley had already translated the Duras biography we would publish in 1994—I can't remember what took so long, but O'Brien was always postponing publications—and I think we asked if he'd be interested in translating the Crevel, which had been recommended to us from someone. (I wish, not for the first time, I had kept a journal back then.) I remember working into the night in the Naperville office, my desk spread with his translation, Rattray's suggestions for improvement (he admitted the translation got better as it went along), a copy of the French original, and my Cassell's French dictionary, trying to finesse the tricky prose. As a result, I was delighted when *Publishers Weekly* called it "beautifully written and beautifully translated."

Jack Green, *Fire the Bastards!* (1992, Introduction by SM). There's a long story behind this caustic critique of the reception of Gaddis's *Recognitions* in 1955, for which see the book's introduction. Without informing me, Dalkey reissued this in paperback in 2012, complementing their reprints of Gaddis's first two novels the same year, with a puzzling new cover: a macho photo of Gaddis supplied by his daughter Sarah. Nor did I learn until a decade later that the book was published the same year in a Spanish translation (*sin mi introducción*).

Alexander Theroux, *The Lollipop Trollops and Other Poems* (1992). Theroux's 1981 novel *Darconville's Cat* swept me off my feet, and I had been a fan of his work ever since. He wanted too much money for paperback rights to that, and so, eager to publish something by him, I accepted this collection. When bound galleys were ready, he asked me to send one to critic Camille Paglia for a blurb. She sent back an angrily handwritten letter scolding me for intruding on her time, telling me she doesn't approve of blurbs, and claiming she threw the galley in the trash. Theroux's response was to add the vicious if cleverly titled "Passacaglia for an Italian Witch," dedicated "For Camille." Having a cover donated by his friend Edward Gorey helped immensely: we distributed a poster version at the ABA convention that summer, and the limited edition signed by the artist and the author sold out quickly. See my *Alexander Theroux: A Fan's Notes* for more on the book, and for my failed attempt to publish a collection of Theroux's fables the following year.

Felipe Alfau, *Sentimental Songs* (1992). I believe critic Ilan Stavans recommended this, which we accepted just to get all of Alfau into print. He was fascinated by Alfau's story, began researching and writing a biography, and apparently obtained from him this thin collection of poems, originally written in Spanish (*La poesía cursi*, literally "corny poems," a title that Ríos pronounced "perfect"). We published it as a bilingual edition, the only one we ever did. Ilan wrote the introduction and translated the poems; we later learned that Alfau disliked his translations.

Jacques Roubaud, *Hortense in Exile* (1992). A sequel to *Hortense Is Abducted*, and even more fun to work with because it contained lots of tricky typography and other postmodern bells and whistles. I came up the name WHortense for the sleazy Wrong Hortense (Dom had simply used Fake Hortense), and received the author's permission to insert a photograph of him and his cat that he complained his French publisher wouldn't allow (p. 160). There's another black cat on the cover, but not mine.

Djuna Barnes, *Ladies Almanack* (1992, afterword by SM). I wanted to follow *Ryder* with this jeux d'esprit, and asked the Authors League for permission to reprint the brief foreword Barnes wrote for the 1972 Harper & Row reprint, but they refused, telling me NYU Press was planning to reissue it (as they did later in 1992). I explained that since the book itself was in the Public Domain, we planned to go ahead with it (minus the copyrighted forward), and they responded with bullying, self-important letters dodging the question of copyright, which we ignored. Like *Ryder*, it did well: we reprinted it three years later, and Dalkey has kept it in print—with cover changes—ever since. (I haven't checked to see if my afterword is still there.)

Olive Moore, *Collected Writings* (1992, Appendix by SM). Back when I was still at Rutgers, Dalkey author Tom McGonigle asked if I had ever heard of this pseudonymous British author from the 1930s—he had come across an intriguing entry on her in a reference book—and once I started reading her I decided we must return her to print. At that time O'Brien was contemplating doing omnibus editions, and since Moore's three novels were relatively short, he agreed to let me compile such a volume. Moore also wrote a short nonfiction book—bitter, aphoristic comments on modern life—and I convinced O'Brien to let me squeeze that one in so that we would have her complete works in one volume, which came to only 426 pages. I wrote Susan Sontag asking if she would be willing to write a blurb; she declined, and asked if I was related to Miss Moore. Gore Vidal in Italy said he'd take a look, but never responded to the bound galley I mailed him. Of all the

authors I "rediscovered," she may be my proudest, and in recent years
Moore's work has been the subject of many essays and dissertations.
Dalkey issued the best novel, *Spleen*, in paperback in 1996, the same
year that Serpent's Tail in England reissued her second best, *Fugue*.

Robert Coover, *A Night at the Movies* (1992). I had been a fan of Coover's
ever since I read *The Public Burning* in 1977, and when I learned that
this collection of short stories was o.p., I jumped on it. Later, I wanted
to reprint more novels by him, but O'Brien was lukewarm about him,
having once written a dismissive review of his *Spanking the Maid*.
As I wrote in part 1, I'm proud of the cover I created for this (p. 19).

Ewa Kuryluk, *Century 21* (1992). When this arrived, O'Brien passed
this along to me (perhaps saying "This looks more like your kind of
book," as he occasionally did), and it blew me away. Kuryluk was a
well-known Polish writer, artist, and art historian who began writing in
English only a decade earlier. As I copyedited it I occasionally corrected
minor slips of the sort made by ESLs, but otherwise left it alone. I
designed the interior, including the photo gallery at the end, but she
did the cover (one of her own artworks). I met her a few times, an
intellectually intimidating cosmopolitan and way smarter and cultured
than I was. This was the only novel she ever wrote.

David Markson, *Collected Poems* (1993). This one was done as a favor
to one of my favorite authors, though I do like the poems. Most of
them were written in Markson's forties and fifties, and I had to work
to stretch the manuscript into 96 book pages, achieved by adding
essays Markson had written in 1973 on two poets he had known,
Dylan Thomas and Conrad Aiken.[4] The cover photo (p. 47) was taken
in Mexico in 1959.

Rikki Ducornet, *The Jade Cabinet* (1993). My favorite of hers: see part 3.

Joseph McElroy, *Women and Men* (1993). I attended the publication
party for *Women and Men* in May 1987, reviewed it in the Fall 1987
issue of the *Review*, had my picture taken with McElroy in 1988 at Brad
Morrow's fifth anniversary party for *Conjunctions* (held at Joe's loft;
see http://www.stevenmoore.info/photos.shtml), edited a special issue
of *RCF* devoted to him (Spring 1990, about which we corresponded
voluminously), and consequently suggested we reprint *Women and
Men* after it went out of print. O'Brien wagged his head in woe at the
anticipated printing bill for the 1200-page book, but said OK. His agent
balked at our request for a permanent license—necessary to uphold

---

4 I always wanted to reprint *The Collected Novels of Conrad Aiken*, but can't
remember why I didn't. I think it had something to do with his estate; we had no
end of trouble with literary estates.

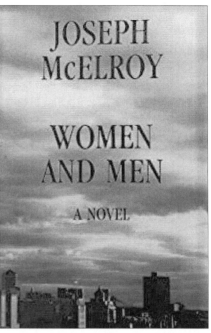

our commitment to keeping our books permanently in print—granting us instead a 10-year license, "stamped all over," she assured us, with a commitment to renew it. Ten years later, they decided not to, partly at Joe's wish to give the book a new start elsewhere, which led to years of o.p. status until Dzanc did a small paperback printing in 2018, keeping it only intermittently in print thereafter.

Carole Maso, AVA (1993). I had known of (if not yet read) her earlier novels published by North Point Press, and when O'Brien and I traveled down to Illinois State University in mid-January 1991 (just when U.S. forces began bombing Baghdad) to meet some of the faculty in a restaurant, we were introduced to their glamorous writer-in-residence. At one point Carole asked if she could send us two recent manuscripts that North Point had turned down, and when they arrived O'Brien turned them over to me for evaluation. I liked them both, especially the more experimental *AVA*, which she had recently finished, and we signed up both of them. She wanted to publish that one first, before the earlier-written *American Woman in the Chinese Hat*. The copyediting went smoothly, though I remember instinctively correcting "Vence" to Venice, only to have her inform me that Vence is a small town on the French Riviera. (But she decided to keep Venice anyway!) Between the galleys and the finished book she altered the ending, and she chose the cover art. She was delighted at my suggestion to reproduce it on the endpapers as well, resulting in a beautiful book. Largely on the basis of *AVA*, she was awarded a Lannan Literary Fellowship for Fiction in 1993.

Carole left ISU in 1992, and when Charlie Harris asked if I knew of anyone to take her place in the creative writing department, I recommended a very creative writer named David Foster Wallace. When Carole returned to the campus a year or two later, she posed between O'Brien and me for the accompanying photo.

Paul West, *Words for a Deaf Daughter* and *Gala* (1993). My two favorites from the prolific British author, one nonfiction (1970), the other a fictional sequel (1977), ingeniously structured and scientifically informed. West liked the idea of reprinting them in the same volume and wrote a preface for it. O'Brien didn't care for West because Sorrentino didn't, and he tended to ape his idol.

Jacques Roubaud, *The Princess Hoppy, or, The Tale of Labrador* (1993). Mentioned and pictured earlier, this was submitted to us by translator Bernard Hœpffner. It was too whimsical for O'Brien's taste, so I handled this one, with pleasure. (In general, he liked novels that exposed the ugly side of life.)

In addition to this and the two Hortense novels, we published three other books by Roubaud during my time there, but they were more John's than mine, though I copyedited, designed, and saw them through production. *The Great Fire of London*, a complex 330-page novel, was published in 1991, which O'Brien worked on as much as I did. Years later, unsatisfied with Di Bernardi's translation, he published a slightly revised version, along with translations of later novels in the Great Fire of London cycle. While I was still there, we also published two collections of prose poems about the death of the French Oulipian's wife, *Some Thing Black* (1990) and *The Plurality of Worlds of Lewis* (1995), both translated by Rosmarie Waldrop. I dutifully copyedited them and designed suitably mournful covers, using black and white photos supplied by the author, but I'll leave them in O'Brien's column.

Marguerite Young, *Miss MacIntosh, My Darling* (1993). See part 3.

Lauren Fairbanks, *Sister Carrie* (1993). O'Brien had accepted Sorrentino's recommendation that Dalkey publish Lauren's slim book of poems, *Muzzle Thyself*, in 1991, though he turned the actual editing and production over to me. I attended the reading she gave at a Chicago bookstore in the summer of 1991, where her mother took our picture (see p. 40). I liked her style and asked her if she had written, or considered writing a novel, and year later she sent me this bizarre, linguistically supercharged novel, and said, in the copy she signed for me, that I was her intended reader, which touched me. Aside from light copyediting, the only suggestion I made was to move a passage near the end to the final page, which Lauren went along with.

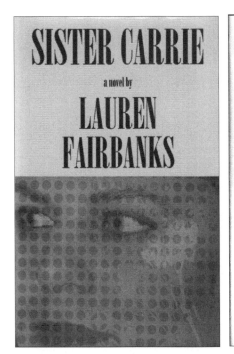

But I've never been happy with the design. She wanted to set the book in a sans-serif font like Helvetica, but literary novels rarely do so; I ran Lauren's suggestion by O'Brien, who agreed we shouldn't, but now I wish we had. She sent me a photo she wanted to use for the cover, but I didn't know what to do with it, and eventually came up with something too elegant for such a rambunctious novel. I wish I had used that image for something resembling a punk-rock concert announcement from the late Seventies: individual letters clipped out of various magazines and newspapers, pasted together like an old-fashioned ransom note, with a photocopy of that image set askew, printed on orange or acid green paper. Ah well. We got some great blurbs for the novel—from Alexander Theroux, Paul West, Larry McCaffery, Lance Olsen, Ellen G. Friedman—but not from Dave Wallace, who told me he threw the bound galley against the wall in exasperation and asked me to explain, as to a fourth-grader, was going on in the novel. I couldn't; it's not that kind of novel. Though I encouraged her write more, Lauren took twenty years to complete another novel, the even stranger *SUPERPOWERS(S.)*, and another seven years to get it into print (2021). She tells me she's working on something new, and I can't wait to see it.

Raymond Queneau, *Saint Glinglin* (1993). Early on, O'Brien had acquired and published several novels by this French polymath (*Pierre Mon Ami, Odile, The Last Days*), but he turned over to me James Sallis's translation of this erudite satire on anthropology, folklore, philosophy, and epistemology, which became my favorite of all our Queneaux. I hardly needed to touch Jim's excellent translation, but I did manage to improve on the crucial final paragraph. However, I made one major error, which bugs me to this day. Queneau had self-imposed the Oulipian constraint of using no words with the letter x (unless unsounded in a character's name) until the final word of the novel, but while going over the proofs one last time before sending it to the printer, I noticed a word that looked slightly off, and after locating it in the French original and consulting my French dictionary, I thoughtlessly changed it to "inflexible" (p. 7). A few weeks after the book came out, someone called the office to ask if that was a typo. (Who does that!? *Some* people, obviously.) I left behind a note to correct it when/ if Dalkey ever reprinted it, which they did ("infleggsible") in 2000 when they issued a paperback edition—with a cover I had rejected and left in my files: it was striking but misleading, too surrealistic, and in vibrant color when we were still wedded to black and white covers. My cover was, how you say, *médiocre*.

Julieta Campos, *The Fear of Losing Eurydice* (1993). I think la Ducornet suggested that her Denver University colleague Leland H. Chambers send this translation to me. At any rate, I copyedited it and oversaw the complicated interior layout, and chose the cover image, which looked to me like a ballet version of the Orpheus and Eurydice myth. In truth it was just an excuse to use a photo I had purchased years earlier of a hot Joffrey Ballet dancer (Leslie Carothers, not the guy). I contacted the photographer, Herbert Migdoll, obtained his permission, and paid a fee. But a few months later I received a letter from Ms. Carothers telling me that a friend had brought the cover to her attention and, while flattered, chided me for not obtaining permission. I told my queen that I had indeed obtained permission, which she could verify with Mr. Migdoll—who, a few months after publication, sent me an invoice for the photo. I had to remind him I had already paid him. It's a lovely book, inside and out.

John Barth, *LETTERS* (1994). I had been a fan of Barth's ever since reading—nay, devouring—*The Sot-Weed Factor* in my early twenties, and read *LETTERS* (all caps, he reminded people) when it first came out in 1979. (That was when I owned my own bookstore and could get any book I wanted wholesale.) It was o.p. by the early 1990s, so I asked for and received reprint rights. Barth advised me on the correct edition to use (Fawcett Columbine, 1982, which corrected errors in the first edition) and wrote a brief foreword for ours. I like the cover I designed (as did Barth's agent), but I wish I had obtained a higher-res copy of the image, and reproduced it in color.

Carole Maso, *The American Woman in the Chinese Hat* (1994). This was the third novel she wrote though fourth to be published. The main thing I remember is the trouble we had with the cover designer, Nicolas Africano, a friend of the author's based in Normal. We had the book ready for the printers, but he kept us waiting; he finally showed up at our office one morning and created the cover on Shirley's computer in a half-hour's time. Carole says I did the handwriting, but it must have been based on something she supplied. Though she said she liked the cover, the ad director for a gay magazine was indignant at the image I sent him, which doesn't reproduce well. A much more accessible novel than 1993's *AVA*, Plume bought paperback rights and issued it in fall 1995, with a prettier but inappropriate cover art (Klimt's *Danae*). Along about then Carole offered her new book *Aureole* to us, and while I loved this erotic story sequence, and later wrote about it,[5] she was disappointed at O'Brien's new policy of publishing new books only in paperback, so she took it to Ecco, who published it in hardcover in fall 1996. She includes me in the acknowledgements, and I *strongly* identify with the protagonist of "Dreaming Steven Lighthouse Keeper."

Rikki Ducornet, *The Complete Butcher's Tales* (1994). See part 3. The manuscript (and bound galleys) ended with "La Chincha," but Rikki agreed with my last-minute suggestion to end the published volume with "Voyage to Ultima Azul, Chapter 79" and furnished an evocative tale-piece illustration for the final page. Dalkey brought out a paperback edition in 1999, with two new stories added at the end.

Aurelie Sheehan, *Jack Kerouac Is Pregnant* (1994). In 1992, Aurelie submitted to *RCF* a story with the arresting title "Jack Kerouac Is Pregnant," under the assumption we were a fiction journal. Before returning it, I read the story and liked it so much that I asked if she had enough stories for a book that *RCF*'s book publication arm could publish. Soon she sent a manuscript of fourteen stories and a novella, four of which had been published in journals—including the immortal *Gutter Poodles*—and O'Brien allowed me to offer her a contract. My editing was minimal: I pointed out one POV violation and suggested placing the novella last rather than earlier, to which she agreed. I didn't care for the cover art she submitted; I had a Robert Longo image I wanted to use instead (see p. 18), but I deferred to her wishes. Jerome Charyn and Carole Maso supplied blurbs, and I noticed that two years later Carole included a character named Aurelie in one of the stories in her fabulous *Aureole*. For her debut, Aurelie received the Jack Kerouac Literary Award, aptly enough, and her next two books were scooped up by Viking.

Desmond MacNamara, *The Book of Intrusions* (1994). An Irishman of many skills—sculptor, art professor, theater and costume designer,

---

5 "A New Language for Desire," *RCF* Fall 1997, rpt. in *My Back Pages*, 660–67. I enjoyed Carole's company on several occasions, sometimes with her partner Helen Lang, and we've kept in touch over the years.

book reviewer—MacNamara (1918–2008) hung out with writers like Flann O'Brien and Brendan Behan, and was even the basis for the character MacDoon in J. P. Donleavy's *The Ginger Man*. Getting wind of us somehow, perhaps because he designed the original cover for *The Dalkey Archive* at Flann O'Brien's request (and which I would have used for our 1993 reprint had I known of it then), he mailed us this, his first novel, in 1992, and I told John we should do it, for it was in the same vein as *At Swim-Two-Birds*. I don't remember making any changes to the text, and he supplied the cover art, of course (his own), and his old friend Donleavy sent us a lovely blurb. MacNamara published a second novel in 2006, *Confessions of an Irish Werewolf*, which has become quite rare. I wonder if it was ever submitted to Dalkey.

Janice Galloway, *The Trick Is to Keep Breathing* (1994). At an ABA convention in 1992 or '93, I met with a Scottish publisher who gave me a half-dozen recent novels to consider for U.S. licensing. When I got home I went through them, and was gobsmacked by this novel, published in 1989, which won several awards then. Rights were secured, some typos corrected, a so-so cover created (from a portfolio of photos a woman once gave O'Brien), and we published it in 1994. It got great reviews here—the *Times Book Review* said, "The book resembles *Tristram Shandy* as rewritten by Sylvia Plath"—and we reprinted it in paperback the following year with a better cover. On the basis of this novel, Galloway was given the E.M. Forster Award by the American Academy of Arts and Letters, and invited to come to New York City to accept it. With O'Brien's encouragement, I flew out there to accompany her, then learned too late that she couldn't find a babysitter! I attended the ceremony anyway, with Brad Morrow and Carole Maso, and introduced the latter to William Gaddis, the last time I saw him.

In 1998, I was astonished to see that my favorite new rock group, Garbage (fronted by a redheaded Scottish hellion named Shirley Manson), had a song on their new album entitled "The Trick Is to Keep Breathing," based on Galloway's novel (per the liner notes). For me, that beat the E. M. Forster Award.

Geoffrey Green, Donald J. Greiner, and Larry McCaffery, eds. *The Vineland Papers: Critical Takes on Pynchon's Novel* (1994). Despite what it says on the cover, this was edited by Green and me. A year or so after *Critique* (edited by all three) published a special issue on *Vineland* in 1990—consisting of the first five essays in this book— Green contacted me about publishing an expanded edition, which as a Pynchon devotee I was eager to do. He gathered most of the other essays and sent them to me, while I suggested two others: I wanted to

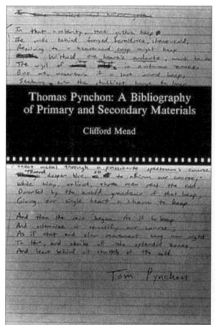

reprint an essay by Joseph Tabbi (then a friend) that had appeared in the *Michigan Quarterly Review*, and I asked Cliff Mead to prepare a bibliography. Green left the actual editing of the new essays to me. I limited myself to routine copyediting for most of them, but made major cuts to Andrew Gordon's fascinating memoir at the end. The original was much longer due to background material about his life in the 1960s, which I felt would be of little or no interest to readers. I didn't ask Gordon's permission, violating my usual dealings with authors. I didn't want to argue, or risk him pulling the essay from the collection. It was reprinted in *The Portable Sixties Reader* (Penguin, 2002), and Gordon eventually published the uncut version on his website.[6]

I designed the book as well. The page layout followed that of *Vineland*, and the film sprockets on the cover were obviously inspired by the section dividers in *Gravity's Rainbow*, which I had used earlier for Cliff's book. The cover image was taken from the inside back cover of a large anthology called *The Movement toward a New America*, edited

---

6 As an editor, I was harder on contributors to the *Review* than on Dalkey's authors: the latter were creative artists, the former mostly academics, whom I held to a different standard. Though still comparatively hands-off, I felt more at liberty to edit some articles and reviews into publishable shape, and even—on rare occasions—rejected a contribution.

by Mitchell Goodman (Pilgrim Press, 1970). The photo credit says it was taken at the Kent State massacre in 1970. We published this as a split edition—maybe 300 hardcovers and 1500 paperbacks—and I'm pleased to see this has become a collector's item among Pynchonites.

Marguerite Young, *Angel in the Forest*; *Inviting the Muses*; and *Marguerite Young, Our Darling*, ed. Miriam Fuchs (all 1994). See part 3. Miriam Fuchs had co-edited *RCF*s Fall 1989 issue on Kathy Acker, Christine Brooke-Rose, and Marguerite Young. For *Inviting the Muses*, I was aided by the most beautiful intern Dalkey ever had, a young woman named Lori Itano (already married).

Ronald Firbank, *Complete Plays* (1994, Introduction by SM). A companion volume to the short story collection we did in 1990. Only one of the three plays included here was previously published; the other two were edited from manuscripts provided by university libraries. I *so* wish we had reproduce the images of Princess Zoubaroff on the front and back covers in color. Quartet Books in England made arrangements with us to combine both the stories and plays into a volume called *The Early Firbank*, with an introduction by Alan Hollinghurst, whom I met while at Rutgers and who provided me with the names of anonymous *TLS* reviewers for my Firbank bibliography (see below).

Wilfrido D. Nolledo, *But for the Lovers* (1994). A 1970 novel by this Filipino-American recommended to me by Robert Coover: See page 18. The cover was created by Tamara Fox, a friend of Angela's, I believe. She also did the vibrant color cover of Queneau's *Saint Glinglin* that I rejected.

James Merrill, *The (Diblos) Notebook* (1994). An experimental novel I read years earlier, which O'Brien OK'd—largely, I suspect, because it might give him access to the Merrill Foundation. (It didn't.) Offset from the 1965 original, the novel is rife with typographical high-jinks; the printer even called me up to ask if a passage set upside-down was meant to be that way. The cover image was sent to me by Alan Ansen, an old friend of Merrill's. The poet wrote a new preface for the book, and died a few months after our edition came out.

Arno Schmidt, *Collected Early Fiction, 1949–1964* (1994–1997). See part 3.

Christine Brooke-Rose, *Amalgamemnon* (1994). I believe it was Ellen J. Friedman, co-editor of *RCF's* Acker/Brooke-Rose/Young issue, who recommended we reprint this 1984 novel, and having read several of the British writer's novels in the 1980s, I was pleased to add this brilliant experimentalist to our list. See page 18 for the cover I came up with. I remember exchanging a few letters with Brooke-Rose, who was living in France, but no more than that memory.

Ellen J. Friedman and Richard Martin, eds. *Utterly Other Discourse: The Texts of Christine Brooke-Rose* (1995). Friedman offered this as a companion volume to the novel above—the source of the title—which I copyedited, but I let someone else design the cover, with brilliant results (see p. 27 above). As I said in part 1, O'Brien took an irrational dislike to it. I know that Friedman (or maybe someone else) recommended we reprint another Brooke-Rose novel because I remember seeing it on his messy desk, but this brainy woman was more my type than his and Dalkey never did another of hers.

Djuan Barnes, *Nightwood: The Original Version and Related Drafts*, **ed. Cheryl J. Plumb** (1995). Given our previous Barnes reprints and a special issue of *RCF* devoted to her (Fall 1993), Professor Plumb approached us with an elaborate variorum edition she had prepared, and which *Nightwood*'s publisher, the esteemed New Directions, would allow us to publish as long as it was hardback only. I love scholarly editions of classics and jumped on it, and even helped Plumb with the Explanatory Annotations (pp. 211–31). It was a bear to design and for Shirley to typeset, but I enjoyed every minute of it.

Louis-Ferdinand Céline, *London Bridge* (1995). Julián Ríos recommended this to me, a long novel that picks up where the shorter *Guignol's Band* leaves off. Rights and funding were available, and Dom Di Bernardi got to work on it. O'Brien had been complaining about the quality of his translations, so I worked extra hard to make this as good as possible (once again with the original and a French dictionary at hand). O'Brien read some of it, and called me into his office, but after I shot down his first four or five lame objections, he paused, then dismissed me. Annoyed that some of our previous translations had been criticized, he was actually annoyed at the praise this one got, and said the reviewers didn't know what they were talking about! (Again, he didn't read much of it.) I modeled the interior on the Gallimard original—this time, I was the thief—with the same heavy Bodoni font they often use for their literary titles, but a few years later, when Dalkey brought out a paperback edition, O'Brien had it reset in what looks like Garamond and in a smaller point size, so that it was around 60 pages shorter, lowering printing costs slightly. I have received praise for the cover, as simple as it is; the jaundice-yellow type really pops.

Christopher Sorrentino, *Sound on Sound* (1995). After striking out everywhere else (some 30 publishers, he later wrote), Gil's son submitted this to us, which we were happy to take on because it was just the sort of inventive, experimental novel that we favored (unlike those other 30). O'Brien turned it over to me to edit and design, which I enjoyed because it was whip-smart and dealt with rock music. Chris

was easy to work with; we collaborated on the interior, he designed the front cover, and his mother took the author's photo on the back. I don't know why Dalkey never reissued this in paperback, which most rockers favor over poncy hardcovers.

Severo Sarduy, *Cobra* and *Maitreya* (1995). I admired the Cuban's strange novel *Cobra* (1975), and reviewed his related novel *Maitreya* for *RCF* (Summer 1989), both short enough to combine into this twofer. I asked James McCourt, my favorite gay novelist, to write an introduction, and then created one of my better covers, from an illustration I found in some book. I assumed it was a drag queen, but years later discovered it was the Russian-American silent-screen star Alla Nazimova, the lead in a film version of Wilde's *Salomé* that I owned!

Carol Ann Sima, *Jane's Bad Hare Day* (1995). I loved this comic surrealistic novel about a forty-something divorcee in Manhattan; O'Brien didn't read it but gave me the go-ahead as long as I "believe in it," a reasonable criteria he often used. We were both disappointed to learn the author was using a pseudonym—he more than I, in fact he wanted to cancel the contract—which the author adopted because she was a school teacher then and didn't want to risk retribution. By now she's surely retired, so I don't think it does any harm to reveal for the record that her real name was Carol Essner, a charming, confident redhead I met during one of my trips to New York. She supplied (maybe drew,

I can't remember) the cover art, which Angela predicted bookstore buyers wouldn't like. "I have to sell this!" she huffed. Carol went on to write one more fanciful novel, *The Mermaid That Came Between Them*, published by Coffee House Press in 2002.

Rikki Ducornet, *Phosphor in Dreamland* (1995). I have especially fond memories of this one: see part 3.

Rikki Ducornet, *The Stain* (1995). Reprinted from the error-filled 1994 original edition; errors corrected by me, cover by someone else.

Jerome Charyn, *The Tar Baby* (1995). I've always been attracted to novels in nonfiction form (travel guides, dissertations, dictionaries,

academic biographies, etc.—I've got a Wallace-length footnote on these in volume one of *The Novel* [pp. 580–81]) and thus got a kick out of this novel in the form of a college literary quarterly, first published in 1973. To further the conceit, I modeled the cover on a recent issue of *RCF*.

Janice Galloway, *Foreign Parts* (1995). Published the previous year in England, I wanted to bring out a U.S. edition of this road novel—not as experimental as her last one, but just as impressive. I couldn't find a satisfying image for the cover, so I let someone else do it (the back cover credits Adam Strong), with inappropriate results since the novel takes place in France, not in a hallucinatory desert. I should have kept looking, or paid to use the superior British cover.

Michel Butor, *A Portrait of the Artist as a Young Ape* (1995). Someone submitted a partial translation of this short novel, which I knew about from the Roudiez book we published years earlier, and quickly cottoned to because of its exotica and *Arabian Nights* intertextuality. Since it was a French translation and underwritten by the French ministry, O'Brien OK'd it without even reading it, as I recall. He knew Butor's earlier novels, which was sufficient. But then something went wrong: the translator changed his mind and withdrew it, or disappeared, and so with the contract deadline approaching I asked Dom Di Bernardi to complete it, and then went back and altered the first guy's translation for consistency with Dom's continuation. I enjoyed copyediting it, but in my rush I used Burton's translation for the *Arabian Nights* quotations rather than, as I realized later, Mathers' English translation of the French Mardrus edition, which is what Butor would have used. The cover, not done by me but which I liked, harkens back to Dalkey's old black-and-white covers.

Karen Elizabeth Gordon, *The Red Shoes and Other Tattered Tales* (1996). My annotation grew so long that I decided to move it to part 3, q.v.

Susan Daitch, *Storytown* (1996). As I said at the end of part 1, I liked the few short stories Susan had published by 1993, so a year or two later I invited her to send us a book's worth. I liked the collection, but O'Brien didn't; he read it and compiled a two-page list of what he regarded as errors and slips—both by the author and by me, for failing to catch them. I sent the list to Susan and she defended nearly every one of her choices, to my satisfaction if not O'Brien's. As I said earlier, I trusted authors knew what they were doing and tended to keep my hands off, he didn't and was eager to "correct" them.[7] I designed the interior of the book and solicited a fine blurb from Dave Wallace, who called her "one of the most intelligent and attentive writers at work in the U.S. today." I introduced them to each other at a Dalkey-sponsored party during the 1992 MLA Convention in New York, the first time I met either of them in the flesh. In 2002 Dalkey issued a paperback edition of her first novel *L.C.*, which I had reviewed in the Fall 1988 *RCF*, but that was probably at the prompting of another editor than O'Brien.

Steven Moore, *Ronald Firbank: An Annotated Bibliography of Secondary Materials, 1905–1995* (1996). I'd been working on this side project for years, and since Dalkey had already published two scholarly bibliographies—Cliff Mead's Pynchon in 1989, and McPheron's Sorrentino in 1991 (see below)—I asked O'Brien sometime in 1995 if I could publish this, offering to pay the productions costs and waiving royalties, allowing Dalkey to keep whatever meager sales the book might generate. He agreed. But in January, after I submitted my resignation, he saw the title on our spring list and slipped a memo under my door accusing me of pulling a fast one, and that the manuscript should be submitted for consideration, like any other book, and for a place on a future schedule. In a memo I left on his chair—we were barely speaking at that time—I reminded him of his earlier agreement, and pointed out that it would be infinitely easier for me to wrap up this vanity project before I left. He relented, claiming he had forgotten, so I had Shirley flow it from my computer disk, which made it quick and easy, designed a simple but elegant cover—a Wyndham Lewis portrait of Firbank—and sent it off to the printer, only to discover when I received finished copies in May that Shirley had accidentally lopped off the last line of my preface (which should conclude ". . . date due to a surge of new material"). There's a rule in publishing that the day you receive a finished copy of your book, you'll open it up and spot a typo. But I was happy just to be done with it. The book received a few nice reviews, including one from Michael Dirda in the *Washington Post*, and managed to sell nearly 200 copies over the years, not bad at all for a book like this. And in the contract, which O'Brien waited

---

7 This from a man who never published a book of his own, only a collection of interviews with Black writers (1973) that he later admitted he fudged with, inventing and then supplying questions and answers, or rewriting their responses to better reflect his views. I was aghast at his confession, but he saw nothing wrong with the procedure. He started but never finished a book on Sorrentino; it probably would have been pretty good, if his long, introductory essay in the Sorrentino issue of *RCF* is any indication.

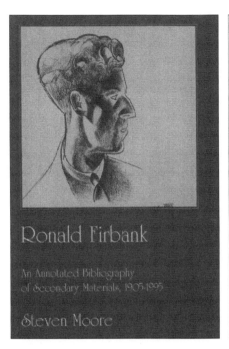

until June 10th to sign, he even allowed me to collect royalties (6% of the list price of $30). So we both profited from it.

John Barth, *Sabbatical* (1996). After reprinting *LETTERS* in 1994, I was eager to get my hands on any other Barths that went o.p., and published this one just before I left, with a spectacular cover by J. Derek Thompson, another freelancer. As with *LETTERS*, Barth wrote a new foreword for it and corrected errors in the original. Although I don't recall O'Brien ever showing much interest in Barth, I was happy to see Dalkey reprint a few more of his novels in the ensuing years, undoubtedly encouraged by Barth scholar Charlie Harris, culminating in a splendid hardback edition of his *Collected Stories* in 2015, after which this giant of modern American literature drifted into what Charlie told me was a "mental twilight."

Fernando del Paso, *Palinuro of Mexico* (1996). Ilan Stavans recommended this huge, Shandyesque novel, first published in Mexico in 1977, then in an English translation by Elisabeth Plaister by Quartet Books in England. Given a chance at selling U.S. rights, they were happy to send me a copy, and I was very happy to read it, one of those big, eccentric, encyclopedic novels I live for. But I had noticed many typos, so as I prepared it for our printers, I had to have Shirley strip in dozens and dozens of corrected lines over the Quartet version. One example I've never forgotten: at one point, mention was made of a "sand clock." *¿Qué?* I located the sentence in the Spanish version, saw that the original phrase was *"reloj de arena,"* then learned from my Spanish dictionary that it meant "hourglass"! I found so many similar errors and typos that I asked for and got a discount on our licensing fee. I had great difficulty locating del Paso in Mexico, and our communications via fax were faulty. Then, O'Brien rejected the introduction Stavans had written for the novel, complaining his English wasn't perfect; maybe not, but it was good enough (I don't think I had edited it yet), but he was deaf to my pleas. And *then*, to top it off, Angela arranged for a nauseating cover. (Look it up; I'm not going to befoul my book by reproducing it here.) We received copies of the finished book just before I left. Years later Dalkey published a translation of another huge novel by del Paso called *News from the Empire* (with a striking cover by Danielle Dutton) but O'Brien let *Palinuro* go out of print, abandoned like Virgil's Palinurus.

§

David Markson, *Reader's Block* (1996). The first of a few books I edited, designed, and proofread before I left, with everything ready for the printer. By 1995, it had been ten years since Markson finished *Wittgenstein's Mistress*, but in December the manuscript for this novel landed on my desk. I stopped what I was doing, sat there and read it straight through, reached for the phone and called the author, and when he answered, said, "David, you have written another master-piece." I passed it along to O'Brien, who approved it (though I don't know if he did more than flip through it), and added it to our Fall 1996 list. I copyedited it—lightly, for Markson carefully prepared his manuscripts—and had Shirley typeset it. Worried at its length, David asked me to make it over 200 pages, which I did (somewhere around 220), but when O'Brien saw it, he ordered me to make it shorter. (It came in at 198 pages, saving Dalkey maybe a whopping $300 in printing costs.) I was around long enough to see the bound galleys, and was delighted at its dedication page: "For Steve Moore and Jack O'Brien / Reader's keepers." All was well, I thought, when I moved back to Colorado in August 1996.

In September, disaster struck. I got the details from Stacy, and then from David. In the process of moving around the book descrip-tion on the back cover, a forced endline hyphenation (such as mat-/ erials) was bumped to the next line, with the hyphen still intact (as in "incontestably fascinating mat-erials"), which nobody noticed. When David received his finished copies, he spotted the error and lost it.

Late that night (or early the next morning), he called Dalkey's office and left a message about the error. Then another message, stating how important it was to correct the error. And a third, and maybe a fourth. By the time he called again, O'Brien had arrived at the office, learned of the error, and screamed at David "Don't ever call this number again!" and hung up. He probably printed 5000 copies, and to his credit didn't shrug off the admittedly minor flaw. He had to correct the back cover and either pulp the entire first printing (which would have been in the warehouse by then), or ship all 5000 back to the printer and have them strip off the old cover and replace it with a new one. (I don't know which option they chose.) In addition to correcting the glitch, he had Todd Bushman revise the cover, for it was slightly different from the flat I'd seen of the original one. And believe me, I took no delight in hearing what happened because I was no longer in charge of such things.

If that wasn't bad enough, another disaster struck five years later, when it was time to reprint it. Apparently Angela Weaser had given a group of interns copies of the first printing and asked them to look for any errors, as an exercise. They found about a dozen things, except that all but one or two were not actual errors. For example, one of the culturally deprived interns came across the name Brünnhilde, looked up the unfamiliar name, came across Byrnhild (as the name is spelled in Norse mythology), and decided Markson had misspelled it, unaware that Markson was referring to Wagner's doomed soprano, not the Norse goddess. David once shared a list of these "errors," but that's the only one I remember, except for the date of the Trojan War: Markson's source may have said it occurred in the 13th century BC, while an intern came across someplace newer that suggested the 12th—ha! another error by the dumb author. And here's the shocking part: instead of running these "errors" past the author, Angela made the changes to the text and sent it off to the printer. It wasn't until David received copies of the second printing in 2001 and leafed through it that one change caught his eye, then another, then he reread the entire book and found the rest. Another raging phone call (or maybe a letter) followed, Angela explained what had happened, and said it was too late to fix. (They weren't going to pulp and reprint the novel *again*.) He told me he became physically ill at the news, taking to his bed. She also first resisted, then agreed to delete O'Brien's name from the dedication. (I don't have a copy of the second printing; the third simply states "For Steven Moore.") It wasn't until 2007, when a third printing was needed, that he called the current managing editor, explained the situation, and had the errors removed, except for a few unimportant ones that he acquiesced to (like maybe the contested date of the Trojan War). As a public service, anyone coming across the unauthorized second printing of 2001 should destroy it on sight.

O'Brien's uncontrolled outburst to Markson was another shooting-himself-in-the-foot move. Had he controlled his temper, he would have had access to the three subsequent novels David published between 2001 and 2007, which he published with Counterpoint instead, not to mention the earlier Markson novels they have reprinted over the years.

Julián Ríos, *Poundemonium* (1997). Again translated by Richard Alan Francis in collaboration with Julián. A short novel in which three characters from *Larva* react to news of the death of Ezra Pound, this was a delight to work on. I suggested the title "Parting Shots" for the last section (*Notas de desdoblamineto* in the original). After this came out, Knopf picked him up for a few wonderful novels (*Loves That Bind*—which I reviewed in the *Washington Post*—and *Monstruary*), then Ríos returned to Dalkey a decade later for two more translated books, his first novel *Procession of Shadows* and his tour-de-force critifiction *The House of Ulysses*. In March 2000 I visited him at his beautiful home outside Paris—the photo was taken by his wife Geneviève Duchène—and we've remained in contact ever since.

Roger Boylan, *Killoyle: An Irish Farce* (1997). This hilarious, foot-noted novel was submitted to us in 1995, edited and designed by me in 1996, and was ready for the printer sans cover when I left in

June. I later learned from "Blazes" (as we called him at the office) that when O'Brien got around to reading it, he told him he didn't like the ending and pressured him to rewrite it, which Boylan did. (Someone also tarted up the running heads for the revised version.) *Killoyle* got great reviews and sold well: it was reprinted only a year later—very rare for our books—translation rights were sold to a few foreign publishers, and it attracted the attention of Grove Press, who published a brilliant sequel entitled *The Great Pint-Pulling Olympiad: A Mostly Irish Farce* (2003), which contains a playful reference to Dalkey's Angela Weaser (". . . the year Angela's Wheezer won at Fairyhouse" [70n11]). The third novel in the trilogy, *The Maladjusted Terrorist*, has not yet appeared, though it was translated and published in Germany in 2007.[8]

W. M. Spackman, *The Complete Fiction* (1997, "Afterword" by SM). I had been savoring Spackman ever since 1978's *An Armful of Warm Girl*, and in 1984 was asked to support his nomination for an honorary degree at the University of Colorado, where he once taught. (I was told my letter was especially effective.) I had wanted to do this omnibus ever since he died in 1990. I obtained permission from the Spackman heirs, wrote what I consider one of my finest introductions, Shirley typeset the book, interns helped proofread it, and Stanley Elkin supplied a stupendous blurb just before he died in 1995, calling it "as distinguished and significant a publishing achievement as the publication in 1946 of *The Portable Faulkner*." But O'Brien, unfamiliar with and indifferent to Spackman's work, kept putting it off. It wasn't until I mentioned that the Spackman family was wealthy and would probably be willing to partially underwrite it—negotiations began right after I left in June 1996—that the book was finally published the following April. I was so *persona non grata* at that time that no one at Dalkey informed me of its publication, or sent me copies or any reviews (of which there were plenty, including a fine one in the *New Yorker* by John Updike, who called my afterword "excellent" ☺). I had to buy a copy at the Borders bookstore at which I was then working, and special-ordered one of the library-intended hardbacks (priced at $44.95; I still have the receipt, which says I got a 10% employee discount.) Also, I was annoyed to see that my introduction had been moved to the back of the omnibus as an afterword, and a footnoted

---

8 I can't resist noting that, years later, Boylan wrote a very flattering review of the second volume of my history of the novel: "The Big Dig," *Boston Review*, 17 March 2014: https://bostonreview.net/articles/roger-boylan-steven-moore-novel-alternative-history/.

page reference screwed up in the process.[9] I came across an early bound galley with the introduction still upfront, and later learned that O'Brien felt my intro was too scholarly and would scare off readers. I guess I should count myself lucky he didn't delete it altogether. During my final years at Dalkey I also prepared the manuscript for a companion volume of Spackman's complete essays, but I wasn't able to publish that for another twenty years, by which time the *Complete Fiction* was out of print.

Emily Holmes Coleman, *The Shutter of Snow* (1997). Because of my interest in Djuna Barnes, a young academic named Marisa Januzzi suggested we reprint this 1930 novel by a friend of Barnes. I liked it, O'Brien accepted my recommendation, and that's where things stood when I left. But soon after, Marisa told me that O'Brien had rejected her introduction to Coleman's novel; Marisa had been reviewing books for me for a few years by then, which were smart and well written, so I can't imagine what the problem was. She regretted recommending it, and threatened legal action, but she wasn't in a position to do so. The novel was published in August 1997 without an introduction, depriving readers of much-need context, keeping only Marisa's uncredited "About the Author" note at the end.

§

In addition to the above, there are books that were offered to and accepted by O'Brien that he turned over to me to see through the press, such as:

Viktor Shklovsky, *Theory of Prose* (1990). O'Brien was tantalized by the few chapters from this key work of Russian Formalism that were translated into English by Richard Sheldon and Robert Sherwood starting in the mid-1960s. As soon as he founded Dalkey, he began bugging Sheldon for a complete translation of *Theory of Prose* (the expanded 1929 edition), but he was dragging his feet for some reason. Consequently, when a translator named Benjamin Sher proposed a Russian translation of something or other in 1989, O'Brien asked him if he would translate Shklovsky instead, and he agreed. Sher threw himself into the task, and O'Brien read and criticized chapters as they came in, but when Sher was finished, O'Brien turned the thing over to me, which became the hardest book I've ever had to copyedit. Many authors are quoted, especially Russians ones, and

---

9 The footnote on p.12 originally referred to a page in the introduction, and should have been changed to p. 621 in the afterword, but someone typed in the utterly meaningless "p. 213."

while Sher used available English translations when he could, in some cases he simply translated block quotations directly from the Russian. It took me an entire afternoon to locate a particularly puzzling passage in Dickens's *Cricket on the Hearth*. I spent several days at the University of Chicago library tracking down references, verifying quotations, and compiling a bibliography as best I could from Shklovsky's offhand references. I never did identify Vladimir Peretts's *Istochnik skazki*, for example. (This was pre-Internet, of course, but I just spent fifteen minutes searching online and *still* can't find it.) Typesetting the book wore Shirley out. After she finished typing the bibliography, filled with entries like "Zelenin, Dmitry. *Velikorusskie skazi permskoi gubernii* [Great Russian Tales of the Perm Province]. St. Petersburg, 1913," she literally got up and walked around to recover. And then I created the index, which was tedious (as indexing always is) but I felt necessary. So while O'Brien adopted this wild child, I cleaned it up and made it presentable—and even quote from it in my later work—and thus am tempted to claim partial ownership.

No sooner was it published than Sher started sending in revisions, which we stripped in for the first and subsequent paperback editions. Years later, O'Brien commissioned a new translation, which was finally published in 2021—but without a bibliography or index. Slackers.

William McPheron, *Gilbert Sorrentino: A Descriptive Bibliography* (1991). Sorrentino was definitely O'Brien's author: he devoted the first issue of the *Review* to his brilliant oeuvre, inaugurated Dalkey Archive Press with a reprint of Sorrentino's *Splendide-Hôtel*, and became his principal publisher in 1987 after North Point Press dropped him due to poor sales. I shared his admiration for Sorrentino: after reading a selection from *Mulligan Stew* in the aforementioned *In the Wake of the "Wake,"* I read the newly published novel itself, was dazzled by it, then sought out his earlier novels and read new ones upon publication. His *Rose Theatre* (1987) was the first Dalkey hardcover I purchased, and I beheld with awe the immaculate manuscript of its sequel, *Misterioso* (1989), for which I designed the cover and wrote the jacket copy, based on Gil's suggestions.

But O'Brien knew McPheron's scholarly bibliography was more my kind of thing, so I saw it through the press, and thus sort of consider it one of "mine," if anyone's. Bill's manuscript was near-perfect and required almost no help from me; he even supplied the cover art. (He was the librarian at Stanford who had purchased O'Brien's archives around 1988, and another batch in the early 1990s.) Speaking of Sorrentino:

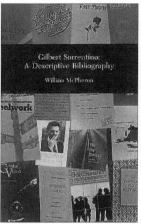

Gilbert Sorrentino, *Under the Shadow* (1991). After presumably reading
it, O'Brien handed this over to me. I copyedited it (which barely needed
it), designed the interior with some chapter title decorations that Gil
liked very much, and did my best with the cover: the proprietors of
the image—Joseph Cornell's *Allegory of Innocence*—insisted that it be
reproduced as it: we couldn't superimpose type over it, or even crop
out the picture frame. (As I've been writing this, I've been re-reading
Ulysses and was reminded that "under the shadow" comes from the
Scylla and Charybdis chapter of Joyce's novel [9:164], and refers
to the shadowed portion at the rear of an Elizabethan stage.) I told
the author that its vibe reminded me of *Twin Peaks*; he admired the
show, but asked me not to make that comparison in the jacket copy.
The book went off to the printers, in plenty of time for its November
15th pub date.

Sorrentino arranged for a reading in Palo Alto—he was teaching
at Stanford—and whoever sponsored the event placed a large order
for books ahead of that date, which we forwarded to our distributor.
The date approached, and the sponsors said the books hadn't arrived,
even though I knew that they had arrived at our distributor—a small
company run by one guy and a few part-timers. (We ran through a
number of distributors in those days, none satisfactory.) Turns out
the distributor filed their order away with other pre-orders, but forgot
to check his file when *Under the Shadow* arrived, and started filling
only new orders. We didn't learn of this until a day or two before the
event, by which time it was too late. Sorrentino was understandably
furious with us, as furious as we were with our distributor (whom
we dropped shortly after), and Gil decided that he would never trust
Dalkey again with a new book. He allowed O'Brien to continue

reprinting his older titles as they went o.p.— I designed covers for *Steelwork* and *Imaginative Qualities of Actual Things* to match that of *Under the Shadow*—but denied him the honor of publishing any of the half-dozen new books he would go on to write. I read each as it appeared—I especially liked the hilarious *Gold Fools* (2001)—and Gil and I still got along on a personal level. He commiserated with the troubles I was having with O'Brien, for he too had been losing respect for him over the years, especially for the way he referred to his ex-wife, whom Gil had liked, as did I.

Ford Madox Ford, *The March of Literature* (1995). It was O'Brien's idea to reprint this huge survey of literature, and my idea to get Alexander Theroux to write an introduction for it. As a small, nonprofit press, Dalkey didn't pay authors for introductions to our reprints, who wrote them pro bono, but knowing that Alex was out of work at the time, I told him we'd pay him $500, then wrote a check to Dalkey for that amount so that he wouldn't know it came from me—otherwise he would not have accepted it. I read the entire 900-page book and liked it very much, and later quoted it in my own work.

Gertrude Stein, *A Novel of Thank You* and *The Making of Americans* (1994, 1995). Around 1993, Stein scholar Steven Meyer suggested we reprint some of Stein's novels, and offered to write introductions for them. Though neither O'Brien or I had a particular interest in her, we acknowledged Stein's importance and figured her name would make a good addition to our list. Since I saw both through the press, they probably belong in my column. After familiarizing myself with Stein's publication history and learning what was out of print, I suggested starting with *A Novel of Thank You*—written in the mid-1920s but published posthumously in 1958—because I found it appealing *plus* it had never been released in paperback, only in the multivolume hardback *Yale Edition of the Unpublished Writings of Gertrude Stein*. We offset their edition and I designed what I considered a pleasing cover (which Dalkey ditched when reprinting it years later).

Then we decided to take on the mammoth *Making of Americans*, for which Meyer wrote another fine introduction, and William Gass a not-so-fine foreword (which, as I mentioned earlier, he came to dislike: I think he felt rushed). I read the first couple hundred pages of it, but was not compelled to read on, I'll confess. O'Brien had a copy of the huge (6 x 9) Something Else bootleg from 1966—the novel had been still under copyright (as I later discovered when we were preparing to reissue it), but they neglected to get permission—but since the quality wasn't that great, I actually purchased a rare Boni & Liveright edition for around $700 (one of only 100 copies bound in cloth and exported to the U.S. from the Contact Press edition published in France in 1925), intending to offset that for better quality. Upon receiving it, I was surprised that the text area was much smaller than that in the bootleg, and also realized it was stupid to send such a rarity to the printer, who had to unbind it in order to offset it. So I sent them the Something Else edition with instructions to reduce it by 20% or so to match the original. We published it in 1995 with the gaudy cover described in part 1, and I noticed that when Dalkey Archive reprinted it years later, they blew it up again to 6 x 9—ignorant or indifferent to its original size, which I had followed for authenticity's sake. Since then it's undergone further cover changes. I recall suggesting that if we did another Stein, it might be *Lucy Church, amiably*, which Dalkey did indeed reprint in 2000.

Osman Lins, *The Queen of the Prisons of Greece* (1995). In 1991, Adria Frizzi offered O'Brien her translation of this Brazilian author's short-story collection *Nine, Novena*, which he rejected. (It would be published by Sun & Moon Press in 1995.) But he showed interest in this 1976 novel, which he passed along to me when it arrived. I wrote to Adria in August of the same year and said we'd be happy to publish the novel, and then went to work on it. I copyedited and prepared it for publication, only to have it postponed until the fall of 1995, which synergistically turned out for the best: in addition to Sun & Moon's publication of *Nine, Novena*, the fall issue of *RCF* contained a section on Lins edited by Adria. So even though O'Brien solicited the novel, I did all the work on it; years later, however, O'Brien told Adria that *he* edited the novel, which is contradicted by the paper trail. (This is all from an email exchange between Adria and me in early September 2022—unlike me, she has preserved her paperwork.)

Alf Mac Lochlainn, *The Corpus in the Library: Stories and Novellas* (1996). This scholar-librarian's first book, *Out of Focus* (The O'Brien Press, 1978), had been one of Dalkey's earliest reprints (1985). A decade later he sent us a hilariously learned novella entitled "The Corpus in the Library," which was too short to be published separately. But I really liked it and suggested that we ask the author to send us any other stories he may have written to fill out the book, which he did. I worked with Shirley to recreate the multi-font typographical complexities of the title novella, and was happy with the other, more traditional stories. But after the book was typeset, O'Brien objected to one of them, claiming it was too weak to include. I argued that since the author apparently felt otherwise—else he wouldn't have sent it—we should defer to him. But O'Brien didn't defer to nobody, so out it went. This was the last cover I designed; I found the library

image, and asked Adam Strong to provide a cosmic background. In 2015, Dalkey published the Irish writer's last collection of stories, *Past Habitual*, three years before he died.

§

And finally, I want to mention some later Dalkey reprints that I suspect I was at least partly responsible for. In March 1995 O'Brien asked me to compile a long list of reprint-worthy books that he could present to foundations, especially Lannan, for financial support. I spent a few days going through my home library, and O'Brien's in the office, maybe a few reference books, and checked on the status of the candidates in *Books in Print*. I handed him the list, he glanced over it, said thanks, and tossed it onto his perpetually messy desk. (Mine was always neat.) In the years after I left, I started noticing that Dalkey was reprinting some of the titles on my list, and since I don't recall ever discussing these novels with him, or hearing him say anything about them, I can probably claim these as my progeny:

Brigid Brophy, *In Transit* and *Prancing Novelist: In Praise of Ronald Firbank* (2006, 2016). I had admired this brilliant Englishwoman ever since the 1970s, when I read her huge book on Firbank, which doubles as a fierce defense of artistic (as opposed to naturalistic) fiction, and read several of her novels after that. I edited the section on Brophy in *RCF*'s Fall 1995 issue, and in my brief introduction singled out her novel *In Transit* for special praise. On the other hand, I remember O'Brien had a copy of *Prancing Novelist* on his bookshelf. I was genuinely surprised when Dalkey reprinted that in 2016, for it's an eccentric 600-page book on a writer most people have never heard of, including Dalkey's cover designer, who added "A Novel" at the bottom (currently visible on Amazon; I haven't seen an actual copy). However, after I showed the first draft of this book to Chad Post, a later editor at Dalkey, he informed me that he was responsible for reprinting *In Transit*: he read about it in the *RCF* issue I edited, sought it out, and loved it. But he urged me to retain this entry, perhaps because I was *indirectly* responsible for its reissue. I'll take any opportunity to sing this woman's praises.

Gabriel Burton, *Heartbreak Hotel* (1999). I enthusiastically reviewed the hardcover of this innovative novel in the Summer 1987 issue of the *Review*, and it was one of the first I put on that list. So glad they reprinted it. "They" embraces later Dalkey editors, for perhaps, like Chad above, they discovered this on their own.

Stanley Elkin, various titles. Another writer I began following in the 1970s, and whose books I've reviewed here and there (see pp. 158–63 of *My Back Pages*). At the time I compiled that list, I believe only a few early ones were o.p., such as *A Bad Man*, but I may have added a note saying any of his are worth reprinting.

Steven Millhauser, various titles. As with Elkin, I remember putting this fantasist's name on that wish list, and within a few years of my leaving Dalkey reissued two of his story collections. Before I left I even inquired about publishing the uncut version of one of his novels, perhaps *From the Realm of Morpheus*.

D. Keith Mano, *Take Five* (1998). I read this shortly after it came out in 1982, the same year and from the same publisher as *Darconville's Cat*, and found it a similar tsunami of verbal energy. While at Dalkey I exchanged a few letters with Mano and discussed the possibility of reissuing it someday. I was delighted to see Dalkey reprint it two years after I left, and with an unprecedented introduction by O'Brien himself.

There may be a few more on my list that were reprinted, but I'm content to take conditional credit for these.

PART 3
My Dalkey Authors

With Felipe Alfau and manuscript of *Chromos*,
Queens, May 1991

Felipe Alfau

[As I say below, this was written for the *Review of Contemporary Fiction*'s Georges Perec/Felipe Alfau issue (Spring 1993, pp. 245–47). I entitled it "Recalled to Life," the title of Book 1 of Dickens's *Tale of Two Cities*.]

ALTHOUGH I DIDN'T originally plan to contribute to this issue, my name and that of Dalkey Archive come up often enough that a short note clarifying our part in rediscovering and publishing Alfau seems warranted to set the record straight.

Chandler Brossard is directly responsible for Alfau's rediscovery, but in a more indirect way than he indicates on page 196. When I made contact with Brossard in 1983 and expressed interest in researching his work (which eventually resulted in the special issue of this magazine devoted to him in the spring of 1987), he mentioned some of the articles he'd written in his earlier days. I located his 1972 *Harper's* article "Commentary (Vituperative)," a diatribe against the then-current fiction scene; on the last page, Brossard names the very "few writers whose work I regard as authentically fabulous," including "an almost totally unknown Spanish-American named Felipe Alfau, whose stories *Locos*, printed thirty-odd years ago, are in a class by themselves." We never discussed Alfau, nor did he loan me his copy of the book. But somehow Alfau's name stuck in my mind.

Two years later, in August 1985, I was visiting friends in New England. One of them,[1] Richard Scaramelli—like me, an inveterate book collector— took me to a used-book store in Marlboro, Vermont, called The Bear, housed in a former barn. There I spotted an unjacketed copy of the 1936 edition of *Locos*, and recognized the name from Brossard's article. Since Brossard's taste in fiction is superb, and since the book was signed by Alfau, I figured it was worth the ten-dollar price tag. I didn't get around

---

1 The other was Cliff Mead, whose Pynchon bibliography I would publish four years later (2022 note, as are the ones that follow).

to reading it until early 1988, by which time I was on the staff of Dalkey
Archive. After literally two pages, I knew this was a novel we should reprint;
I showed the book to John O'Brien, founder and publisher of Dalkey
Archive, and he instantly agreed. Since we had an unexpected opening
in our fall 1988 list, we rushed the book into production.

I spent hours in the Rutgers library trying to find out something,
anything, about the author. Aside from a handful of 1936 reviews of *Locos*,
I came up empty-handed. I searched the indexes of the *New York Times* for
an obituary, assuming that the author was probably dead. Then an advisor
to the press, novelist Thomas McGonigle, decided simply to look in the
New Your City phonebook—and there he was. McGonigle called him to
express our interest in doing the book, to which Alfau agreed with some
bemusement, and then I called him to close the deal. I was taken aback
when he refused to accept an advance, so we agreed to use his royalties
to fund the production of similar forgotten books.

O'Brien suggested that we get someone to write an introduction or
afterword, and Mary McCarthy seemed the logical choice since she had
praised the 1936 edition so highly. Somehow I got her Paris address,
wrote to her, and was delighted to have her accept. She no longer had
a copy of the book, so I sent her mine, which she lost when returning
in 1988 to summer in Maine. (Miss McCarthy never did find my copy
of *Locos*; I had to pay $50 for my second copy, though worth it because
it had the original jacket.) I then sent her our page proofs and waited.
The book was announced for October publication, but we didn't receive
her piece until September or so, which pushed the book's publication
back to the end of December.[2] On her own, she placed her essay with
the *New York Review of Books*, which had far-reaching effects. Many of
the contributors to this issue learned of *Locos* there, because it wasn't
widely reviewed elsewhere.

In fact, there were no reviews at all for several months (aside from pre-
publication notices in book-trade journals), but then two splendid reviews
appeared in late spring 1989 that would make a world of difference: Michael
Dirda's in the *Washington Post Book World* and Anna Shapiro's in the *New
Yorker*. These two, along with McCarthy's piece in the *New York Review*,
were not only responsible for bookstore sales, but also for a paperback
reprint sale to Vintage Books and deals with publishers in England, Spain,
Italy, Holland, Germany, and France. (These are the sales, as opposed
to actual bookstore sales in the U.S., that Ilan Stavans is referring to on
the top of page 148 of his interview with Alfau; our "financial troubles"

---

2 But we did have time to add it to the Fall 1988 "Novelist as Critic" issue of *RCF*.

at the time were the usual growing pains of a company expanding from a small one to a larger one, as we did in 1988–89.)[3] All of this attention laid the groundwork for our publication of *Chromos* in 1990, which was more widely reviewed and was also sold to Vintage,[4] England, and many other foreign countries.

I learned of the existence of *Chromos* in 1988 as our edition of *Locos* was in production. Alfau was reluctant to show it to me until he saw how we handled *Locos*: pleased with our edition of that, he sent a photocopy of the yellowing manuscript to me via Daniel Talbot.[5] Contrary to what Doris Shapiro and Felipe Alfau say on page 201, the manuscript wasn't single-spaced (except for the stories-within-stories sequences), nor was it uncorrected: Alfau's handwritten corrections appear throughout. His original title was *Chromos: A Parody of Truth*, which he shortened to *A Parody* when he submitted it. I would have gone along with the original subtitle but didn't feel the shortened one was effective, so Alfau agreed to drop it. (In this and all other matters, Alfau was very cooperative, giving us complete freedom and responsibility for copyediting, proofreading, and design, not so much because he trusted us than because he didn't want to bother with any of it.) Alfau made a gift to me of the yellow manuscript in May of 1991 when I visited him with Ilan Stavans, who took the accompanying photo.

Alfau is joking when he says (on p. 147 of the interview) that he repeatedly asked me to send the negative reviews as well as the positive ones, and that I obstinately refrained from doing so. Truth is, he never asked to see any reviews, positive or negative, nor were there any bad reviews. Virtually every review listed in the bibliography that follows (which includes every review I know of) was positive. The only item I didn't send him was Carol Iannone's "Literature by Quota" (*Commentary*, March 1991, 50–53), which pans all five of the novels nominated for the 1990 National Book Award. I don't take Iannone seriously—she lost all credibility years ago by panning William Gaddis as well—and I doubted Alfau would take any interest in her benighted views.

---

3 Partly true, but Ilan quoted me correctly when he told Alfau, "One of the editors told me that when *Locos* was published, the company was in serious financial trouble. *Locos* helped them recover."

4 Peter Dimock bought it, and later O'Brien published three novels of his. Just before O'Brien went off to breakfast with Dimock in New York during one of our visits, he told me he was convinced Dimock was going to offer him a job at Vintage because of his editorial acumen. He didn't say anything after returning.

5 An old friend of Brossard's, it turned out, bringing things full circle. In the late 1940s both Brossard and Talbot helped Alfau to find a publisher for *Chromos*.

While most editors prefer discovering young writers and nurturing their talent over the years, I prefer rediscovering masterpieces that have slipped through the cracks of literary history. I look forward to watching Alfau's place in twentieth-century literature firm up as more and more readers and critics discover his work. We will lose Alfau one of these days, but we can't afford ever to lose his work again.

Remembering Marguerite Young

[Written for Constance Eichenlaub's "Who Is Marguerite Young?" website, posted 16 March 1999. https://marguerite-young.site/who-is-marguerite-young/board-room-archive/]

I FIRST LEARNED of Young in the early 1970s from Anaïs Nin's book *The Novel of the Future*; her rapturous praise of *Miss MacIntosh, My Darling* led me to pick up the Signet paperback edition, which I soon traded up for a Scribner's hardback. Although I glanced through it over the years, I didn't get around to actually reading it until the late 1980s, by which time I was working for Dalkey Archive Press and its literary journal, the *Review of Contemporary Fiction*. I was the copyeditor for its Acker/Brooke-Rose/Young issue, and working on those essays (and verifying quotations from Young's works) inspired me to begin reading *Miss MacIntosh*.

I immediately fell in love with it. I've always liked big, ambitious books, and have a penchant for what some people denigrate as "purple prose." Needless to say, no one's prose is purpler than Marguerite's! Young magically transformed 1930s U.S.A. into a land of Arabian Nights enchantment, unearthing the dream life of ordinary (and some extraordinary) Americans in a totally unique way. I remember reading it at night, then going to sleep, only to find Young's prose roaring through my dreams. Right around the same time (early 1990s), I received a phone call from a young editor at the New York office of Oxford University Press (whose name escapes me [Tom Burgess?]). He was a huge fan of Young's, knew her slightly, and knew of both *RCF*'s special issue on her and Dalkey's reprint program. He called me to ask if we would be interested in reprinting *Miss MacIntosh*.

I didn't know that the book was out of print then—I thought the two-volume Harvest edition was still available—but it wasn't, and this guy had already talked to Marguerite about Dalkey. I told him yes, we'd love to (at that time Dalkey's editor John O'Brien trusted my judgment on such matters, even though Young wasn't his type of author). So I called Marguerite at the number the friend had supplied and sure enough she agreed. The "business" part of our conversation lasted about five minutes, and then she spent about an hour talking about everything else under the sun, especially people she knew and who admired her work. (She was rather vain in this regard; she made sure I knew she was descended from Brigham Young, relayed her "dear friend" Saul Bellow's opinion of her work to me, etc. etc.). I told her Dalkey didn't have much money to pay for an advance—especially considering the astronomical printing bill that would result—but she said she'd waive the advance as long as we agreed to publish it the way she wanted it: in two volumes. I balked at this because I preferred one big book (like the original edition), but she insisted. She said the one-volume edition intimidated people, scared them off; she wanted something more portable, something people could read on the subway. She was very insistent—in fact said she'd withdraw her offer to let us publish it otherwise—so I relented. In fact, she told me she regretted waiting until the entire novel was finished before publishing it; she wished she had published it in shorter installments throughout the 1950s and early 1960s, the way British writers do (Anthony Powell's *Dance to the Music of Time*, Lawrence Durrell's quartet and quintet, Doris Lessing's Martha Quest series & sci-fi quintet). I remember the title she would have used for the final Esther Longtree section was "Mule." *Miss MacIntosh* contains many novellas within it, and it's interesting to speculate how her reputation might be different had she published them separately.

I had to go to NYC on business in the summer of 1992, so the Oxford University Press contact arranged for me to meet Marguerite at a restaurant in the West Village near her apartment. (It was a diner favored by transvestites; one of them, a rather ditsy-looking blond, greeted Marguerite while I was there, and I later learned that *MMMD* was a favorite of the gay literary community.) Since Marguerite had never signed the contract I'd sent her, I'd brought along another and had her sign it there; she couldn't remember her Social Security number, and after digging around in her purse came up with what later turned out to be her dentist's phone number or something. I'd also brought along my copy of *MMMD*, which she gladly signed, and when I asked if she wanted to make any changes to the dedication page, she said yes and, with my encouragement, crossed out and amended the dedication page in my book, only to decide at the end to leave it as it was. (I didn't mind; I now had a unique copy.) She also gave me a packet of old photographs, which I used both for the covers of Dalkey's edition of *MMMD* (it was my idea to use a "before and after" approach) and for the photo inserts in our later tribute volume, *Marguerite Young, Our Darling*.

The three of us then walked the few blocks to her Bleecker Street address—she held my hand and walked *very* slowly—and up the stairs to her bizarre apartment; books everywhere, boxes and boxes of manuscripts (which she was readying for sale to Yale's Beinecke Library), and countless dolls. I couldn't get much concrete information from her: every question of mine was answered by a flight of fancy that was entertaining but not always informative. (I have to say that she treated the OUP guy rather rudely, ignoring him most of the time when not treating him like a lackey.)

Dalkey published *MMMD* in 1993, with before-and-after photos of the author gracing the covers. (When Dalkey reprinted the volumes at the end of the decade, they replaced my covers with undistinguished ones.) Then I began the three-book project that resulted in the publication in August of 1994 of *Inviting the Muses*, the reprint of *Angel in the Forest*, and

Miriam Fuchs's festschrift, whose covers I also designed. "Negotiations" for these three were pretty casual; Marguerite agreed enthusiastically to the first two, but never returned the contracts I sent her. They arrived just about the time she fell ill and left NYC to return to the Midwest, and apparently were left behind. So I sent a second set to Marguerite's niece (I think; I can't remember exactly who she was staying with), but despite frequent requests, the niece never got Marguerite to sign them. So we published the books without a contract; I had Marguerite's verbal permission, of course, and she was delighted to see the books, so there never was a problem. But still, I felt a bit uneasy about that.

At that time (1994–95) Marguerite began having doubts whether Knopf was serious in its intent to publish the Eugene Debs book—they said it would have to be cut (a knee-jerk commercial publisher's reaction to any long book, it seems)—so Marguerite asked if Dalkey would be interested in publishing the uncut book. After consulting with O'Brien, who by that time didn't trust my judgment as much but saw the publicity value in publishing this "legendary" work, I told her we would indeed be happy to publish it. So Marguerite called Knopf and tried to get the book back, but her editor there (Victoria Wilson) insisted Knopf really wanted to do it, so it stayed there.[6] It was all very confusing; I'd talk to Marguerite on the phone, but she was out of it most of the time, then let a friend or cousin act as middleman, which didn't help matters. And then Marguerite died.

But it's just as well; I left Dalkey in disgust the following year (1996), and since O'Brien wasn't really interested in her work, Lord knows what would have become of it. O'Brien's indifference also led to canceling our contract with Martha Sattler to publish her Young bibliography, which we had announced in several places; O'Brien didn't want to do any more bibliographies or scholarly books (at that time; as was frustratingly typical of him, he changed his mind after I left). And that was the end of my involvement with Young's works, though the prospect of reading the Debs book—finally!—excites me to no end.[7]

I remember Marguerite told me she had come across a few novellas she had written long ago, might even have been sections cut from *MMMD*; I told her Dalkey would love to publish them, but then never heard any more about them. Young's continued neglect is largely due to critics' preconceived notions of canon, genre, etc., which she stands outside of,

---

6 The same editor who insisted on taking Gass's *Tunnel*, only to let it go o.p. a few years later.

7 See *My Back Pages* 380–82 for my review of *Harp Song for a Radical: The Life and Times of Eugene Victor Debs*. See also my review of *The Collected Poems of Marguerite Young* in *Poetry* (posted 3 October 2022).

though anyone who likes Proust and Woolf should be able to read her. I like Eichenlaub's point about "Young's ability to allow imagery to have a life of its own," which accounts for those marvelous flights of fancy that apparently bewildered her reviewers. My favorite example is on the bottom of page 186 of *MMMD*, where the Queen Maud Mountains undergo personification; even though *MMMD* is an intensely serious work, there's a great deal of whimsy in it, which adds to its immense charm.

Coda: Nearly two years after posting the above, I moved from Colorado to Ann Arbor, and while driving across Iowa in February 2001 snapped this photo through the truck's windshield of Miss MacIntosh's hometown. I resisted the temptation to take the exit.

Publishing Rikki Ducornet

[Written for a festschrift on Ducornet published by Verbivoracious Press in 2015, then reprinted in *My Back Pages* in 2017.]

I HAD THE honor of being Rikki Ducornet's publisher during the first half of the 1990s, when she went from a cult author published mostly by small presses to a nationally recognized one published by the major New York publishers.

In 1991 she sent a packet of materials to Dalkey Archive Press seeking a U.S. publisher for her second novel *The Fountains of Neptune*, which had been published two years earlier in Canada. Along with a copy of it, she enclosed the manuscript of *The Jade Cabinet*, along with the latest *Ontario Review* containing a selection from it. I was impressed by *The Fountains of Neptune*, but I really loved *The Jade Cabinet*. After getting the boss's OK, I told Rikki that we would like to publish both right away, so she extricated herself from Ontario Review Press (whose Joyce Carol Oates wanted to publish the new novel) and we brought out *Fountains* in 1992, and *The Jade Cabinet* in the spring of 1993. By then we were already talking about publishing her other works: first an expanded edition of her 1980 short-story collection *The Butcher's Tales*, which we brought out in spring of 1994, and then a corrected reprint of her 1984 novel *The Stain* in the fall of 1995.

Earlier in 1995 we also published her new novel *Phosphor in Dreamland*. That summer, Rikki told us she would be out west and the idea of doing a mini reading tour to promote it came up. By that point I really hated being around Dalkey's publisher and, eager for any excuse to get away from the office, I volunteered to fly from Illinois out to California. Once there, I rented a car and met Rikki for the first time at her son Jean-Yves's place in Oxnard, outside of L.A. I drove her to a daytime reading at Chapman University in Orange (at Mark Axelrod's invitation), and maybe one at Dutton's in Brentwood, another L.A. suburb. I accompanied her to a recording studio where Michael Silverblatt interviewed her for his wonderful *Bookworm* program. Then we drove north to San Francisco. I believe Rikki gave a reading at Black Oak Books in Berkeley, and also at some performance space in San Francisco, where she shared the bill with Dale Peck. (He read from his novel *Martin and John*, which we both found whiny and annoying.) During the early 1990s she occasionally contributed to our journal, the *Review of Contemporary Fiction*, and at my request she did the cover art for our translation of René Crevel's 1933 surrealist novel *Putting My Foot in It*. By 1996 she had caught the eye of the New York publishing world, and the last project I worked on with Rikki was typing up the manuscript of *The Word "Desire,"* which Henry Holt published in the fall of 1997. (Rikki showed her appreciation by dedicating one of its stories to me.) By then I had quit Dalkey and moved back to Denver, where she then lived, and we saw each other occasionally over the next few years. I once invited her to do a reading at the Borders bookstore where I worked, and also interviewed her for a local arts magazine called the *Bloomsbury Review* (January/February 1998).[8] In 2001 I moved to Michigan, but we've kept in touch ever since, and I've read each new work of hers upon publication with deepening admiration.

§

Like many editors, I need only read the first few pages of a work to tell if it's something I want to publish, and *The Fountains of Neptune* quickly seduced me. The sensibility was cultured but unorthodox, the form achronological but cohesive, and the content an intriguing mix of science, psychoanalysis, myth, and fairy tale. But it was the author's quicksilver way with words that did it: after a few more pages I was intoxicated by the colorful, imagistic diction, the Rabelaisian raunch, and the rum-fueled fancy displayed by the denizens of the Ghost Port Bar as they swap increasingly phantasmagoric sea tales. She had me (at page 15) at her description of the sea as "a green-eyed witch; she speaks in tongues," which seemed to describe la Ducornet as well.

For all the whimsy and wordplay, there was also a toughness of mind on display, a blazing intellect stoked by wide reading, a deep contempt for conservative thinking and their repressive institutions, a pro-sex swagger, and an uncompromising allegiance to the unconventional, the heterodox, the subversive. My kind of book, my kind of author.

There was even more whimsy and wordplay in *The Jade Cabinet*, appropriately so in a novel featuring Lewis Carroll. This may be my favorite novel of hers. It is a paean to English eccentricity, but also a

---

8 This was reprinted in *The VP Annual 2016* (Verbivoracious Press, 2016), 81–89.

parable about substantiality vs. ethereality, of commerce vs. aesthetics. Above all, it is an investigation into the mysteries of language, everything from hieroglyphics to muteness. The villain of the piece is a cartoonishly vulgar Victorian industrialist, and the whole thing reads like Dickens's *Hard Times* reimagined by Jorge Luis Borges.

This is the first book of Rikki's that I edited, though "copyedited" would be more accurate, for I did little more than correct a few typos, maybe suggest a few word changes. Unlike some editors who feel a manuscript is unpublishable until they work their magic on it, I take a hands-off attitude toward writers who know exactly what they're doing, as Rikki clearly did. It was fun to work with the graphic elements—handwritten sentences and hand-drawn sketches and diagrams—and Ducornet enlisted the help of her friend Rosamond Purcell to supply the artwork for the cover and endsheets.

I can't remember whether it was my idea or Rikki's suggestion to bring out next an expanded edition of her early short-story collection, *The Butcher's Tales*, which Toronto's Aya Press had published back in 1980 and which Rikki had sent me. Here in miniature were all the qualities I appreciated in her novels, along with excursions into surrealism and science fiction. I deliberately placed at the end an early story that concluded with the lines, "Sleepers awaking, our grey flesh tingling beneath the warm tongues of sister suns, the old dreams stirred; our blood flowed fast now, darkening, already inventing a new language for Desire." That struck me as an appropriately sensuous description of Rikki's whole fictional project: inventing a new language for desire. Most of Rikki's novels have historical settings, set in times and places when "Desire"—not "love" but capital-D *Desire*—was regarded as disruptive and irreligious, a threat to decent society. Rikki respects it for the life-affirming force of nature it is, and in her work finds new, more positive ways to speak of it. We called our edition *The* <u>Complete</u> *Butcher's Tales* because it also included all the stories she had written since 1980, and once again Rosamond Purcell supplied the outré cover art and endsheet illustrations. I remember that, years later, the conventional-housewife publicity coordinator at Borders wouldn't allow me to display it for Rikki's reading because she found the cover obscene.

Shortly after *The Complete Butcher's Tales* came out in the spring of 1994, Rikki sent me the manuscript of her next novel, *Phosphor in Dreamland*, handwritten on legal-sized paper. Previously she had hired typists to prepare her works for publishers, but I volunteered to type this one myself on my newish word-processor, figuring I could copyedit it as I went along. Perhaps because of this hands-on involvement, *Phosphor* remains one of my favorite Ducornet novels. I'm not a quick typist, so the

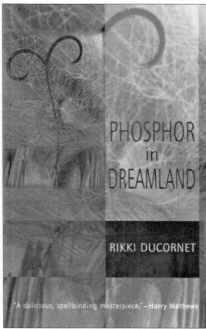

procedure allowed me to savor every word as I went along, to attune myself to her cadences, to trace the twists and turns of her syntax. (Cadence was especially important to her; Rikki rejected a few of my diction suggestions because of rhythm.) There were even more graphic elements than in *The Jade Cabinet*, including a portfolio of drawings we decided to include as an appendix, not something every publisher would allow. I designed the book's interior, and it was my idea to use a tiny seashell for section dividers.

My snail's pace also allowed me to marvel at her manipulation of tone: although the novel is as airy and sunny as its Caribbean setting, it deals with oppression, environmental degradation, religious fanaticism, and madness. The balance between light and dark elements resembles *The Jade Cabinet* in this regard—Ducornet's subsequent novels tip much more to the dark—as does its antiquarianism and natural history excursions. I noted the seamless shifts between the 17th century and the present, and how she used the modern natural history museum as both setting and form—the novel imitates a tour of an exotic museum—and I followed the slowly developing love story between the docent narrator and the artist Polly. (The *Wunderkammer*, or cabinet of wonders, is another model for the novel's form.) I watched how she cleverly worked her interest in Jonathan Swift into the novel, and I recognized in her puritanical "Clean Sweepers" an allusion to the Promise Keepers, a boys-only evangelical Christian group making fools of themselves at that time in Colorado, where Rikki was living. I would have appreciated these things had I simply read the novel, but typing it was like looking over Rikki's shoulder as she composed the work, a Pierre Menard feeling of participating in its creation.

My years at Dalkey Archive were depressing and frustrating, but Rikki and a few other writers kept me sane and entertained. For that reason, I am as grateful to her as she is to me (as she has graciously said) for publishing her works during that crucial period in her brilliant career.

Arno Schmidt

IT WAS WHEN I was a *Finnegans Wake* junkie in the '70s (my 20s) that I began hearing about a gigantic *Wake*-inspired German novel called *Zettel's Traum*—the possessive apostrophe in German is as incorrect as its absence in Joyce's novel—by someone named Arno Schmidt (1914–1979). Published in 1970, it was said to be untranslatable. A few years later I purchased another huge one by Schmidt that had actually been translated (by John E. Woods), *Evening Edged in Gold*, and the following year read Schmidt's contribution to *In the Wake of the "Wake."* So when translator Woods and a representative from the well-endowed Arno Schmidt Foundation approached O'Brien and me at a book convention in 1992 or so, I was all ears.

Woods had spent the last decade translating thousands of pages of Schmidt's early fiction published between 1949 and 1964 (which is when Schmidt began *Zettel's Traum*) as well as his literary criticism. They asked if we would be willing to publish all the fiction and maybe the nonfiction as well. O'Brien also knew the work, for Schmidt had been the subject of the Spring 1988 issue of the *Review of Contemporary Fiction*, guest-edited by F. P. Ott, and I think he may have had owned one or two of the English novellas that were already available, *The Egghead Republic* (1979) and *Scenes from the Life of a Faun* (1983), both published by Marion Boyars (more on whom anon). The Schmidt Foundation's promise of munificent funding sealed the deal for O'Brien.

A little later, a huge box with reams of manuscript arrived; O'Brien asked me to take it from there. (I don't recall him actually reading any of it.) First, I had to decide how we wanted to publish it. The foundation had also sent us the eight-volume paperback "Bargfelder Kassette" edition of Schmidt's early fiction, but I decided to combine them into four volumes, by genre: one volume for the novellas, one for the short stories, one for a trilogy of short novels collectively called *Nobodaddy's Children*, and then two novels, which I imaginative called *Two Novels*. The Schmidt

258 ■ A R N O S C H M I D T

automatically jotted down by mistake as well; (then blow a puff, flatulent=
cheeked tube=mouthed; then brush away the phibrous debris with the edge
of my hand : actually I was far less excited than desirable for lyricull production. Here he came oafing over with the damp glass.) – : "I'll pay now,
okay ?". –
  : "Thunderation ! – Why's that so *cold* ? !". (The change that is, that
he had brought me from my ten-mark bill. He visibly rejoiced behind his
facial flesh at this Little Tryumph; and I let him have some rope; then,
however, admonished him by rapping the table edge with the 1 five-
mark piece : ?). : "Comes outa the freezuh." he proudly retohted; "my wife
keeps a cigahbox o' change in : huh ice=box. – It's huh joke, but of'en
backfuhs". I let him get away with this for once. But now, with more
decamping mind, waved him off again. And then sat there to myself, of
furrowed & allegoric=ferment : didn't it seem as if ideas might be . . . . . ?
. . . – (?) – – : ! :
  : "The lights aglimmer . . . . ."
Nah; wryth=hum too short; ‹I sat, the lights aglimmer› – : ‹swimmer›. Still
too tacitean=terse, the silent man's exit : even the dustiest layerman can
mess=more with longer lines. And y' don't swim at home by lanternlight;
not unless you've got above-average water in your cellar : ‹dimmer› ?, but
that shoots the mood right off. ‹Trimmer›, tree=trimmer : what's my SYN-
TAX have to say ? Grimmer, skimmer, slimmer hymner. So, wrong again;
once a man's past fifty – as usual, there's some US=report or other about it,
not=KINSEY – he has fewer strokes o' genius. But it had a nice hopsy &
blackbrown taste, this cozy mugga beer. – : W=wait ! ‹beer !› –
  :"I sat all cozy drinking beer",
da-dámm da-dámm da-dámm da-dámm : ‹dear› ! :
  "here came my – – uhm – –"
nah; don't use ‹cozy› again) – –
  "here came my happy lad so=dear"
that's it, sure ! (And smile broadly, self=suggestively, 'spite Bismarck &
wallpaper, broader still, to get myself even more sentimental : now hit 'em
with the popular adverbs !) :
  "with arms –"
hm ‹arms› or ‹little arms› ? Can the people, our people, my people digest
yet *another* diminutive ? I would say – ‹yes›. So then run my Faber=point,
run :
  "with little arms to hug me tight."
So that made lines 1, 3 and 4. Which meant, however, that line 2 now
had to rhyme with ‹. . . ight›. – (Justasec. What 'd it all look like up t' this
point –) :

Foundation agreed with my grouping, with one exception—they wanted to move a long story to the novellas volume, or vice versa—and thus we began the four-volume series called *Collected Early Fiction, 1949–1964.*

Almost no copyediting was needed; Woods had worked with advisors from the Foundation, and the text was virtually perfect. (I remember making one correction regarding Schopenhauer's *Parerga and Paralipomena*, but little else.) The main problem were the disks Woods sent us; he used a word-processing program called XyWrite that was unreadable on Shirley's computer. I took it downstairs to the more tech-savvy people at Fiction Collective, and they converted it to files that she could actual read, though they were encumbered by all sorts of HTML-type coding that she had to delete, and then format into odd-looking pages like the one reproduced here (from "Caliban upon Setebos" in *Collected Stories*).

I came up with what I regarded as a Germanic cover design we could use for all four volumes, only needing to switch out the author photos, as well as a promotional leaflet describing the ambitious series. We announced the first volume, *Collected Novellas*, for the fall 1994, and then we ran into a problem. British publisher Marion Boyars got wind of it, and accused *me*, personally, of including *Afternoon of a Faun* without licensing it from her. I wrote back to explain that I hadn't seen that book around for years and assumed it was o.p., but more to the point, the Schmidt Foundation assured us (in their contract) that they owned the rights. So she approached them, and, since our book had already been announced and she had them over a barrel, she extracted a large licensing fee. The *Collected Novellas* was published as planned, and it won the PEN West Literary Award for Translations, among other awards. *Nobodaddy's Children* followed in 1995, which earned Woods the Helen and Kurt Wolff prize, and the *Collected Stories* in December 1996. By then I was gone, but I left behind the typeset pages for *Two Novels*, scheduled for 1997. All that was needed was to correct a few typos and to typeset Woods's excellent introduction. I had also, at O'Brien's request, gone through all the nonfiction—great stuff—and suggested a plan for how it might be published.

But in 1997, trouble struck again, this time from O'Brien himself.

The Schmidt Foundation had generously waived the translator's fee and settled for a standard royalty rate. Prior to the publication of volume 1, O'Brien convinced them to provide $34,000 for "marketing and publicity"—not that it made any difference: *Collected Novellas* sold no better than comparable books of ours published at the same time with no marketing/publicity at all. In fact, O'Brien used only part of the $34K for Schmidt (that leaflet I designed and maybe an ad or two); the rest was used for other things, such as giving his girlfriend Angela a raise.

Prior to the publication of the second volume in 1995, O'Brien approached the foundation again for more money. They were reluctant to do so, for they intended the initial $34K to cover all four volumes, but they eventually coughed up more money. In early 1996, O'Brien—like an obnoxiously persistent beggar—*again* asked the Foundation for money. They initially refused, and O'Brien told me he was tempted to cancel further publication—despite a contract, despite the foundation's previous generosity. Reluctantly they sent him another check.

(As I said, they were well endowed; it was founded by the wealthy Jan Philipp Reemtsma, the victim of kidnapping in 1996; I remember O'Brien growing impatient and insulted when his phone calls to him weren't being returned and, taking umbrage, almost cussed him out as he almost did Charlie Harris in 1992. Reemtsma later wrote an account of his kidnapping, published in English as *In the Cellar*.)

John Woods told me later that after I left in 1996, O'Brien *again* asked for money for the fourth and final volume, *Two Novels*. The fed-up foundation refused, so to spite them, O'Brien sabotaged the book, once again cutting off his nose to spite his face: he refused to include Woods's introduction, jacked up the price to put it beyond the reach of the average reader, short-discounted it to ensure that bookstores wouldn't carry it, and sent the book to the printer with shoddy production values: no jacket copy, no blurbs on the back cover, and a dust-jacket design that

only feebly imitated that of the three preceding volumes. As a result, the book sold poorly, meaning he lost money on the book, and he lost the opportunity to publish further volumes by Schmidt. Beginning in 1999, Green Integer soon published two (out of a projected three) volumes of Schmidt's *Radio Dialogs*, and a brilliant large-format novel entitled *The School for Atheists*. (See *My Back Pages* for reviews of them). And he lost the respect of everyone familiar with his insolent, petulant treatment of one of the greatest German writers of the twentieth century.

Nearly twenty years later, I was doubly surprised to learn that Dalkey Archive would be publishing Woods's translation of *Bottom's Dream*, the allegedly untranslatable supernovel: first, that he had actually finished it, and second, that Dalkey would be publishing it. But I soon learned they would merely be distributing it in the U.S.: the book was typeset and printed in Germany by the Schmidt Foundation, who probably searched for someone else in America to distribute it before settling for Dalkey. I'm sure O'Brien didn't read it, but I did, and since no one asked me to review it—in fact I don't recall seeing *any* reviews in the mainstream review media—I posted a short but sweet one on Amazon.com:

★★★★★ "The charming agonies of Love" (p. 1448)
Reviewed in the United States on October 29, 2016

Verified Purchase

Cuddle up with this sweetly smutty tale of a May-December romance that occupies a midsummer's day and night. A 54-year literary scholar has difficulty fending off the aggressive flirtations of a 16-year-old girl (in the company of her bickering parents); eventually Daniel and Franziska realize their forbidden love is doomed, and part ways.

There is a bunch of other stuff about sex, Edgar Allan Poe, sexual perversions, culture, sex education, Freudian psychology, sexual symbolism in literature, religion, sex and religion, the origin and function of art, and pretty much everything else under the sun. But the funny/sad romance of Dan+Fran lightens the load of encyclopedic erudition, resulting in a piquant German <Lolita.>

(Seriously, though: this is one of the great novels of the 20th-century, and fervent thanks are due to John E. Woods and the Schmidt Foundation for making it available in English.)

14 people found this useful.

Karen Elizabeth Gordon

Karen Gordon's gruesome grammar books would make Strunk and White turn in their graves.

From a feature in *Pulse* magazine, December 1993, taken by Kathryn
Miller at the same session that produced *RCF*'s "Future of Fiction" cover

I HAD BEEN a fan of Karen's Gothic writing manuals (*The Transitive
Vampire, The Well-Tempered Sentence*) and reviewed her *Intimate Apparel:
A Dictionary of the Senses* in *RCF*'s Summer 1989 issue, where I compared
it to Gass's *Willie Masters' Lonesome Wife*, Edward Gorey's abecedaries,
and Milorad Pavić's recently published *Dictionary of the Khazars: A Lexicon
Novel*. (A lucky guess; it turned out that Karen not only loved that novel
but also knew Pavić, and even appears in one of his later fictions.) *Intimate
Apparel* was o.p. by 1993, so that year I wrote to her proposing we reprint

it as a work of fiction, not as a writing manual. (The original pretended to demonstrate how to use certain words in a sentence, but they were unlike sentences any budding author would ever write. Here's her example of how to use the word *towel*: "What are tears? Lock your face in a closet full of towels.") She enthusiastically agreed, and was very impressed by Dalkey's catalog—she loved eccentric French fiction, which she could read in the original—as well as the copy of my review I included, which she had never seen.

Thus began the most enjoyable author-editor relationship of my publishing career. Over the next few years we exchanged hundreds of letters and faxes, not only about her book but about literature in general—she was extremely, exotically well-read—films, music, as well as pages from her various works in progress. (In addition to *The Red Shoes*, she published six other books between 1996 and 1998.) I even got her to review a few books for *RCF*.

Intimate Apparel was divided into two sections of alphabetical words (*absinthe* to *window*, then *babushka* to *zipper*) but since all of her vignettes illustrating the use of those words featured the same colorful cast of characters, I suggested merging the two. She agreed and made some adjustments to original as we repurposed the book, adding and deleting bits, and supplying (I think at my suggestion) a Dramatis Personae up front. At first calling the new version *Tattered Tales*, she expanded it to *The Red Shoes and Other Tattered Tales* because her version of the Andersen fairy tale is scattered throughout the book. She was involved in all elements of design (font, point size, layout) and got her talented friends to supply the cover art and design.

Our pen-pallery was a lifesaver for me. She would send her faxes at night, and I loved arriving at the office and finding one spilling out of the machine, to be savored over my morning cup of coffee before anyone else arrived. As I told her in a fax dated 15 September 1995, "The last nine month have been rather tense and grim around here, and working with you has been the one unalloyed delight and has kept my spirits up." Things got even tenser and grimmer over the following months, but she remained a delight to the end. I was gradually climbing out of my deep depression then, and she played a major role in bringing back into the light.

We kept in touch after I left Dalkey in June 1996. In August I wrote a review for *Rain Taxi* of her *Paris Out of Hand*, which she had written in Paris while we were working on *The Red Shoes*. In October I started working for a Borders store in a Denver suburb, and was shocked to see *The Red Shoes* featured on a sponsored kiosk of curated new books, which must have cost Dalkey a pretty penny; I asked a seasoned employee if those kiosks were effective and he smiled and said no—it was just a marketing

ploy to make money off publishers, not off the books themselves. I met
Karen for the first time when she came to Denver to give a reading at the
Tattered Cover on October 30th. I attended it with Rikki Ducornet, whom
I had visited a few times in her spacious home near Denver University,
where she taught. (It was *très drôle* watching these two American-born
writers converse in French.) Afterward I walked her back to her hotel
downtown, but both of us were curiously tongue-tied, odd after years of
epistolary volubility.

Karen dedicated her 1997 book *The Disheveled Dictionary* to me, and
when she returned to Denver that year, I arranged a reading at Borders on
November 21st, which was a disaster. Only three people showed up, so
they pulled their chairs up to Karen's table and chatted for half an hour.
She was staying with Rikki on that occasion—over the last year they had
collaborated on a book, *Torn Wings and Faux Pas: A Flashbook of Style, A
Beastly Guide Through the Writer's Labyrinth* (Pantheon), and we went
out to dinner one night, along with Rikki's husband. At the end of the
evening I gave her a long hug, and never saw her again.

That month I wrote a Guggenheim recommendation at her request,
but in vain. Over the next few years she told me about various book
projects she was working on—a novel, another faux-travelogue (*Italy Out
of Hand*), a collaboration with writer/illustrator Barbara Hodgson entitled
The Library Amplochacha, even some sort of collaboration with me, but
none of those came to fruition. We kept in touch until 2000, when she
moved to Italy; I told her I would be coming to Paris in March for a Gaddis
conference, and we made plans to meet there, but they fell through. A
decade of silence then followed.

I didn't hear from her again until 2010, when she called to tell me
she liked the first volume of my history of the novel, which had been
published in April. She was living in Washington State at that time, and
we exchanged a few emails and some comically risqué photos (from her,
not me)—then she went silent again.

JOHN SIMON GUGGENHEIM MEMORIAL FOUNDATION
Confidential Report on Candidate for Fellowship

Mr. Steven Moore
103 West Powers Circle, #308
Littleton, CO 80120

Candidate:
Gordon, Karen Elizabeth

472109

REPORT: I am eager to lend my support to Karen Gordon's
Guggenheim application because I've long felt she's one
of the most underrated, yet brilliantly talented writers
in America. Because she has chosen not to write easily
identifiable fiction or poetry, opting instead for fiction
in the form of Borgesian reference books (grammar manuals,
travel guides, etc.), she has been neglected by the literary
community, even that portion that favors innovative, unconventional writing. But in her conceptual daring and bravura
writing, she has proved herself the equal of most of the
innovative writers praised in the review media.

Her proposal to turn one of her best books, Paris Out of Hand,
into a performance piece strikes me as an effective way to
sidestep the hidebound review media and find the larger
audience she deserves. (I am attaching a review I wrote of
the book to indicate why I think both it and Gordon herself
and important.) I have had the pleasure of attending two
of her readings and can attest to her ability to charm and
entertain an audience; the more elaborate performance she
describes in her proposal sounds wonderful. While it may
help Gordon enlarge her audience, the true winners would be
the audience itself: it will see that unconventional, even
experimental writing doesn't have to be solemn, controversial,
or pretentious; that language is a game to be played between
writer and reader (or auditor); and it perhaps will learn
something about French literary culture. A community-based
effort involving actors and audience-participation is a
welcome alternative to the traditional literary reading.

Though Gordon has been writing/publishing brilliant books
for nearly fifteen years, I believe this is the first time
she has applied for a grant, and I hope you award her a
Fellowship she so richly deserves.

Signed _____   Date 23 Nov. 1997

Position or Title _____

Address (if different from above) _____

(Please return to John Simon Guggenheim Memorial Foundation, 90 Park Avenue, New York, N.Y. 10016, at your
earliest convenience. An addressed envelope is enclosed.)

Acknowledgements

I WOULD LIKE to thank the following for commenting on the sloppy first draft, and/or for providing information: Roger Boylan, Maurice Cloud, Adria Frizzi, Jim Gauer, Lauren Jagnernauth, Helen Lang, Carole Maso, Thomas McGonigle, Chad Post, Julián Ríos, Michael Stephens, and one who wishes to be nameless.

Index